PRAYERS

of grief and glory

PRAYERS
of grief and glory

by
Richard Harries

Lutterworth Press
Cambridge

Lutterworth Press
P.O. Box 60
Cambridge CB1 2NT

British Library Cataloguing in Publication Data
Harries, Richard, *1936-*
    Prayers of grief and glory.
    1. Christian life
    I. Title
    248.4   BV4501.2

ISBN 0-7188-2424-5

By the same author
Prayers of Hope (B.B.C. Publications)
Turning to Prayer (A. R. Mowbray)

Cover photo courtesy of Ambrose Greenway

First published 1979
Reprinted 1987

Printed in Great Britain by
The Guernsey Press Co. Ltd., Guernsey, Channel Islands.

For Mark and Clare

I am grateful to all those who through their lives and their writings have influenced my life for good. Others have given me so much. I only hope that through this book some of it is passed on without too much distortion.

I am grateful in particular to Pat McKenroe and Crispian Hollis for their unfailing friendliness and help when these talks were first produced for *Prayer for the Day*; and to Evelyn Wimbush who helped to select and arrange the talks for this book.

RICHARD HARRIES

All Saints' Vicarage,
Fulham.

CONTENTS

THE FAITHFUL WITNESS
OF YOUR SAINTS IN EVERY AGE

FARE FORWARD, VOYAGERS

Out of the Deep

DE PROFUNDIS

Oscar Wilde has a high reputation as a writer of comedies. His plays are still staged and *The Importance of being Earnest* must have brought laughter to millions. But people remember Oscar Wilde as much for his life as his plays. He had an extravagant, often outrageous personality. He didn't fit easily into conventional society which was often shocked by what he said and did. In 1895 he was jailed for two years. Whilst in prison he wrote a long letter which contained these words about Christ, 'By being brought into his presence one becomes something. And everybody is predestined to his presence. Once at least in his life each man walks with Christ to Emmaus.' Emmaus you remember was the village near Jerusalem to which two disciples were walking shortly after the death of Christ when a stranger joined them. On the journey they talked together about recent happenings and at the end, as they blessed and broke bread together, the disciples recognized that the stranger was none other than Christ himself, who at once vanished from their sight. I wonder what it was in his own experience that made Oscar Wilde say that, at least once in his life, each man walks with Christ to Emmaus?

Oscar Wilde loathed prison. He wrote, 'I have laid in prison for nearly two years. Out of my nature has come wild despair; and abandonment to grief that was piteous to look at; terrible and impotent rage; bitterness and scorn; anguish that wept aloud.' Yet during this time he learnt the value of sorrow. He wrote, 'Behind joy and laughter there may be a temperament coarse, hard and callous. But behind sorrow there is always sorrow. Pain, unlike pleasure, wears no mask.' He believed that this sorrow had enabled him to perceive things he had never seen before; that it gave him a more truthful perspective on life. In particular it enabled him to discover in himself what *he* called humility but which is perhaps better described as acceptance of life without resentment or bitterness. 'I am completely penniless, and absolutely homeless' he wrote, 'yet there are worse things in the world than that. I am quite candid when I say that rather than go out of this prison with bitterness in my heart against the world, I would gladly and readily beg my bread from door to door.'

This new way of approaching life, what in fact he called his new life, was related to his continuing reflection on the person of Christ. He wrote, 'Every morning after I have cleaned my cell and polished my tins, I read a little of the gospels . . . It is a delightful way of opening the day. Everyone, even in a turbulent, ill-disciplined life, should do the same.'

Oscar Wilde wasn't a naturally religious person. At one point he wrote, 'Religion doesn't help me. The faith that others give to what is unseen, I give to what one can touch and look at . . . I feel I would like to found an order for those who *cannot* believe.' Yet in prison, reflecting on his own experience and the person in the gospels, he discovered what he felt was a new, more truthful attitude to life. Before he died he was received into the church. In his pain and humiliation he had walked with a stranger whom later he came to see was Christ. I don't think he had what we would call a mystical experience. Rather it was a question of thinking hard about the meaning of his life and what had happened to him, in the light of the gospels. He found that his own dawning insights were both confirmed and deepened by the gospel truths.

O God, grant that as we reflect on the experiences that happen to us your truth and your presence may illuminate our sorrows and our joys.

MONDAY MORNING FEELINGS

I hope it won't be one of *those* mornings, one of those mornings when you feel bored and restless, unable to settle to anything. You know you should start on the washing, but you don't feel you can face it yet, so you do some dusting instead. But after a rather desultory flick round half the room you think 'what the heck' and slump in a chair with a newspaper and a cup of coffee. Or you get to work and though you know you've got four people to ring and a pile of papers to get through it seems a terrible effort to get started on any of it. You keep on delaying, wondering if after all you are not in the wrong job. Or perhaps it comes on when you get back from work. You open the door and down it comes—what someone recently described to me as 'a fit of the bed-sit blues'. The technical name for this state of mind in Christian thought has been *accidie*, and a dictionary gives this splendid definition. '*Accidie* is a state of sad heaviness in which the mind is stagnant and the flesh a burden'.

In extreme forms of course we call this state depression and it needs to be treated by the medical profession. Thankfully people really can be helped these days. But I am not referring to this extreme or prolonged state but to the mood which from time to time descends on us all. And the practical question is what to do about it when it comes. It seems to me the first and most important thing is actually to face up to these feelings we have, consciously to realize that this is what we do in fact feel. Otherwise, what happens? We quickly go and take a drink, or stay on late in the office, or use whatever other device we have ready for battening down the hatch quickly on the bleak waste of our psyche. If you are a praying person you may then turn these feelings into a prayer, as the psalmists did. They are full of phrases like 'why art thou so full of heaviness O my soul, why art thou so disquieted within me?' 'O raise me from these dark depths', prayed Beethoven when he realized that his deafness was incurable. But even if you are not a praying person, or you find it impossible to pray in such moods, the act of consciously realizing what you feel—bored, fed-up, dissatisfied, low or however you describe it—can bring some good. In such a realization we often see through the superficiality of much of our life, and then we see the way towards a more satisfying path. In the darkness, even the terribly mundane darkness of a Monday morning feeling, the divine spirit meets us to lead us on to something better.

Perhaps most important of all, in realizing our own inner bleakness, we become sensitive to the needs of others. For if we reflect on what is most use to us in one of these moods I suspect we would all give the same answer—someone's friendship. The simple act of human kindness, someone being with us, listening or talking, is what helps. In some mysterious way it makes us feel that life has some point after all. As a Jewish theologian put it, 'What do we expect when we are in despair and yet go to a man? Surely a presence by means of which we are told that nevertheless there is a meaning.' He does not mean that the friend talks to us about the meaning of life; rather the actual fact of human contact helps to lift the sad heaviness. Everyone has a problem; almost everyone a secret burden to bear. And most people's problems are not soluble. But what flows between people helps us to go on. Through learning to face and consciously accept our own inner sense of futility, failure or sadness we seem to become more sensitive to the same feelings in others and more willing to reach out a hand to them. I end with a prayer of Tagore.

O God, when my heart is hard and parched up, come upon me with a shower of mercy.
When grace is lost from life, come with a burst of song.
When my beggarly heart sits crouched, shut up in a corner, break open the door, my king, and come with the ceremony of a king.

WHEN SO SAD
THOU CANS'T NOT SADDER

Many people today, particularly those living in urban areas, have a sense of strain. They may feel pressures at work — the sheer number of things that have to be got through in the day, it always seems a fight against the clock; the responsibility that has to be borne, difficult people who have to be dealt with. Or there may be pressures at home. Sick relatives to be cared for; commitments in the local community that can't just be dropped. The result is an underlying sense of strain interspersed with daydreams about retirement to a cottage in the country or a bungalow by the sea. People who live like this need help. But often just because they are the ones most willing to shoulder the burdens of others they are most reluctant to ask for themselves. There may also be another reason. To ask for help, whether from another human being or from God, is to admit our weakness, our helplessness. None of us likes doing this. Yet it's amazing how when we do ask for help it is so often given. The very defencelessness and vulnerability of someone who admits that they can't really cope draws out our most generous impulses.

A similar process happens when a person turns to God for help. Not that God's willingness to give depends upon our willingness to ask — of course not. But our capacity to receive does depend upon having enough humility, even brokenness of spirit, to be able to ask. And those who do ask for help in coping, do receive. They discover within them a power beyond their own power. The tight little ego which usually drives us on is deluded in thinking itself self-sufficient and beholden to nothing. And as soon as it admits its weakness and dependence on something beyond itself all the unconscious resources of our personality are put at its disposal. God wants to act through the whole of what we are, not just our conscious minds and driving wills. When we turn to God for help we allow him to act through the whole of us.

You may remember the famous story from the beginning of the Old Testament when Jacob had a dream about a ladder going from earth to heaven and on this ladder were angels going up and down. Through this picture Jacob tried to convey his sense of God's presence. This image was used again in the gospel of John to refer to Christ as the revealer of God's presence. There is also a third usage in a poem by Francis Thompson. The poem begins by saying that there is an invisible world all about us that most of us are unaware of. It is closer to us than our own souls but, as the poem goes on,

'Tis ye, 'tis your estranged faces,
That miss the many-splendoured thing.

But (when so sad thou cans't not sadder)
Cry; — and upon thy so sore loss
Shall shine the traffic of Jacob's ladder
Pitched betwixt Heaven and Charing Cross.

What is interesting about this poem is Francis Thompson's belief that it is when we are at the end of our tether, when all our human resources have given out and we turn in desperation to something beyond ourselves for help that the divine glory breaks through to us. As he puts it, 'But (when so sad thou cans't not sadder) Cry'. The other point of interest is that this divine presence breaks through to us not just in lonely or beautiful places but in the middle of the busy, jarring tension-full modern world. The ladder reaches to heaven out of the world of strain and pressures — 'betwixt Heaven and Charing Cross', he says, and we might add, 'betwixt Heaven and Birmingham, Liverpool, Glasgow and Belfast'.

O God, our strength and help, as this day with its pressures and problems begins, we open ourselves to you. Grant us powers beyond our own powers that we may spend and be spent in the ways of love and goodness, Through Jesus Christ our Lord.

THE TOAD WITHIN US

The other evening at a party I was speaking to a bus driver about his work. Perhaps I was wrong. Perhaps I should have let the poor chap leave his workday cares behind for a few hours. But we parsons do such a strange job I can rarely resist the temptation of finding out how others spend their working hours. Besides, for many this is the most important part of their life. Their work is what really switches them on. Even if it doesn't, if it is a great burden, it's as well to know how they feel. So, my bus driver friend told me about his day. It seems to me that anyone who has to drive a double-decker through today's London traffic with all its rush, noise, aggro and perpetual possibility of accident must come home with their nerves worn to a frazzle. But my friend didn't feel like this about his job at all. 'No rush', he said. The great secret was to approach the day in a cool methodical way. 'It's like playing a game of chess', he said, 'you inch the big bus out into the stream of traffic, you wait, you judge when the time is just right to move out further—you move.' I suspect that most of us would be too terrified to move at all. Or if we did it would be all flap, jerk and jolt. But not my friend. There's someone who obviously finds a lot of satisfaction in his work.

Yet for all of us there are moments when it all seems a chore, nothing but a long grind. And for some their work is so utterly uncongenial it's as much as they can do to get themselves off in the morning. In one of his poems Philip Larkin likens work to a toad squatting on his life. He wishes he could use his wit as a pitchfork to drive the creature off. He wishes he had the courage to shout, 'Stuff your pension'. But he hasn't. This view of work would certainly have the sympathy of the writer of the book of Genesis where Adam is told that his work will be toil and sweat. For so many millions alas, in the past and today, their work has been just this—a form of slavery.

So it's encouraging that with education and computerization there is now less sheer drudgery to be shared out. It's good too that more firms are now talking about job satisfaction. Not before time. The conditions under which we do our work do need to be changed so that more people can find more fulfilment from what is after all the best part of each day, for the best years of their life. But when change has taken place there is no getting away from the fact that our own attitude to work does vitally affect the matter. Larkin's poem goes on to record that there was something toad-like within him, which kept the toad work weighing his life down. That bus driver's outlook was so different. 'No rush', he said, 'it's like playing a game of chess'. And after he had spoken to me I was reminded of that poem of George Herbert, which you may know as a hymn,

Teach me, my God and King,
In all things thee to see;
And what I do in anything
To do it as for thee!

A servant with this clause
Makes drudgery divine
Who sweeps a room, as for thy laws,
Makes that and the action fine.

FEELING FOR OTHERS

I read a rather sad story the other day. A doctor working in a unit dealing with accidents to the brain became so depressed by the sights he had to see that he killed himself. Every day he had to treat people whose brains were badly injured as a result of car smashes and eventually he could bear it no more. This highlights a problem which now bothers quite a number of sensitive people. Every news has the familiar catalogue of bomb explosions, strikes, accidents and famines. If we allowed ourselves to feel every woe we hear about—for example the grief of a Belfast mother who has lost a son as though it were our own son—we literally could not take it. So most of the time we hear the news with the mind, but we don't take it in emotionally. And on TV especially, the rapid change of programmes helps to keep the shutters up over our feelings. A horrifying documentary on drought in the Sahara will be followed by a cowboy film; pictures of people injured in wars, by a quiz game. This makes it all bearable, but it leaves ordinary people, with ordinary decent feelings, pretty uneasy.

Wilfred Owen was perhaps the best of the poets who wrote about the First World War. He served in the Manchester Regiment and was killed by machine-gun fire in 1918. How well he knew this problem! 'My senses are charred', he wrote once; 'I don't take the cigarette out of my mouth when I write "deceased" over their letters.' In his poem, *Insensibility*, he begins by saying how lucky are all those who can cut themselves off emotionally from the pain around them.

Happy are men who yet before they are killed
can let their veins run cold
Whom no compassion fleers.

Happy are those who lose imagination:
They have enough to carry with ammunition.

18

But then in the final verse he fiercely rounds on this line of thought,

But cursed are dullards whom no cannon stuns,
that they should be as stones:

By choice they made themselves immune
To pity and whatever moans in man.

To remain human we must allow the door to our feelings to remain open. Yet there is another aspect of the matter, no less important. When we go and see a doctor what do we really want? Oh, I know it helps if they have what's called a good bedside manner, if they appear sympathetic. But what matters is that the ailment is correctly diagnosed and treated, and in order to do this a doctor must have a measure of detachment and coolness. He or she needs to be able not so much to feel as to think, to act rationally in our best interests.

God, I believe, combines both boundless sympathy and perfect rationality. Every human sadness and pain he feels with us, as though it were his own. But he also stands outside our situation, able to see and work for our best interests. T. S. Eliot had an arresting phrase in one of his poems. He calls God 'the wounded surgeon.' We are made in the image of God and we are being transformed more and more into his likeness. This means being able both to extend the range of our sympathy beyond the immediate family circle and to take thoughtful, disciplined action on behalf of others. But we are not God. There is a limit to what we can feel, and to what we can do. Here again is one of these tensions, ambiguities, unsolvable problems that we have to live with. To remain human is to remain vulnerable. But to be of use we have to turn some of our feelings into thoughtful, disciplined action in certain chosen areas. We cannot be wounded surgeons for the ills of the whole world. But there will this day be something we will feel, on which we can take some thought and action, however small it might seem.

O God, enable us to feel without being crushed, and turn our feelings into action for the well-being of others, and the glory of your holy name: through Jesus Christ our Lord.

SECURE IN OUR OWN WORTH

As the final stage of Jesus' ministry began, he set his face resolutely towards Jerusalem. On the way he had to pass through Samaria where, because of a slightly different religion, there was hostility to Jews. Jesus sent messengers ahead to make arrangements but the Samaritan villagers wouldn't have anything to do with them. According to the New Testament account 'When the disciples James and John saw this they said "Lord, may we call down fire from heaven to burn them up?" But Jesus turned and rebuked them, and they went on to another village.' This story vividly pictures a reaction familiar to all of us. We are rejected, or feel ourselves rejected, and we immediately want to flay out. We may not want to call down fire from heaven but we certainly want to lash out with our tongue and often do. What is even worse is that we don't always wait until we are rejected before getting bitter; we anticipate rejection. A man once had a flat tyre but when he went to put on the spare could not find his jack. Up the road was a house, so he started to walk towards it with a view to borrowing one. On the way, as one does, he started to daydream of what he was about to do. When he actually got there, and rang the bell, the door opened and he found himself blurting out, 'You can keep your thumping jack, I don't want it anyway.' Going into a new situation, where we don't know what people's reaction will be, always makes us somewhat anxious and insecure. This insecurity makes us anticipate rejection.

People sometimes become, as they say, paranoid. They think others are plotting against them or getting at them somehow. We've all felt like this at times. We pass someone in the street and they ignore us (in fact of course they just haven't seen us). We remember why an old friend was very off hand the night before. We wonder if everyone is dropping us; we wonder what we've done to offend them. We suddenly feel isolated, insecure, edgy and our very tenseness invites the rejection we have imagined.

The word 'insecure' seems to recur. If we were really secure within ourselves would we be able both to stop anticipating rejection and also to cope with it without flaying out, as Jesus did? It seems to come back to having a sense of our own worth. I'm fond of the rhyme about Little Jack Horner,

Little Jack Horner sat in a corner,
Eating a Christmas pie;
He put in his thumb, and pulled out a plum,
And said, 'What a good boy am I!'

Jack Horner obviously had a sense of his own value, a feeling of well-being. Alas, so many people don't have this sense, or only rarely. But God's grace can put right what is defective in our makeup. God's grace can repair our nature, and God's grace can break through to us at any time. Paul Tillich once wrote, 'Grace strikes us when we are in great pain and restlessness. It strikes us when we walk through the dark valley of a meaningless and empty life. Sometimes at that moment a wave of light breaks into our darkness, and it is as though a voice were saying: "You are accepted. You are accepted, accepted by that which is greater than you, and the name of which you do not know. Do not seek for anything; do not perform anything; do not intend anything. Simply accept the fact that you are accepted".'

Grant us, O God, such a sense of our own value that we may convey to others a sense of theirs.

SOULS TO MAKE

A lady came up to me not long ago and said she had never been bored in her life. Alas, this is not the experience of some others for whom it is an almost permanent condition. For example when Graham Greene was a young man he took up Russian Roulette. He put a bullet in the chamber of a revolver, spun it, placed the barrel against his head and pulled the trigger. He says he then experienced a marvellous sense of jubilation at finding himself still alive. So much so that he became hooked on this potentially fatal game and repeated the experiment several times—until he realized that even this no longer gave him a thrill. He wrote about this curious episode, 'one campaign was over but the war against boredom had to go on.' So he became a writer in some of the most dangerous places in the world. 'It was', he said, 'the fear of boredom that drove him there'.

Another novelist, Evelyn Waugh, seems to have suffered boredom of the same intensity. But the distractions he used to ward it off always disappointed. A friend recalls seeing him sitting sadly in a London club. He had called for a bottle of champagne but when it arrived he just looked at it gloomily and said, 'it sounded as though it was going to be jolly and then somehow it isn't.' It may be that boredom is not a strong enough word to describe this state of mind but nor is the medical term depression entirely adequate, though some people who feel like this certainly do benefit from medical treatment.. The old word is *accidie.*

This state of mind seems to be part of our human condition and not just an illness for two reasons. First, many people begin to feel bored and restless when they first sense that life is a serious business; that there is a path of duty to follow and that it is childish to opt out. When Evelyn Waugh was a young man he belonged to a high spirited, high living set—drink parties, fun, more drink, more fun. Then he was converted and religion became the most important thing in his life. He now knew that life was not just for kicks; that eternal salvation, as he put it, was at stake; that there is a daily struggle to overcome the manifold temptations of the world and the flesh, never mind the devil. Although not everyone is religious as he was most of us wake up to the fact that life is a serious business (which is not the same thing of course as saying it has to be lived solemnly). And the struggle to live as we know we should often puts a strain on the system which shows itself in various ways.

The other reason why many people experience this state of sad heaviness has simply to do with the fact of getting older. We can't do all that we once took in our stride. An active person who has become housebound and blind for example is deprived of much of the stimulation which was once life and breath to them. However kind friends are, there is no getting round the fact that life is difficult and at times, sad-making. There is a poem of R. S. Thomas in which he describes lonely parsons in isolated country parishes. He writes

Lost parishes, where the grass keeps
No register and life is bare
Of all but the cold fact of the wind.

This poem begins

There are places where you might have been sent
To learn patience, to make your soul
In long hours. . . .

It's an old fashioned phrase that, isn't it? 'To make your soul.' But don't we all, in one way or another, have to do just that? In a moment of courage, or in long years of a duty secretly done, or a burden borne, we make our soul. And it's not so grim as it sounds. For we are not just animals, here to pleasure for a moment and perish for ever. We have a soul to make; that's why life is at once so hard and so marvellous.

We bless your holy name, O God, that you have given us souls to make. Give grace this day to all who are finding life difficult, through Jesus Christ our Lord.

NO STERNER SORROW

A young man, tired of life in a big city, sought solitude in an isolated village. It was in India and the village was very different from what he had known previously. He found the people strange and the noises at night disturbed him. His one comfort was a cheerful 12 year-old child who looked after the house in which he acted as village postmaster. The girl was an orphan. She had no one to look after her, and she earned a meagre living by looking after successive occupants of the house. Between this girl and the man there grew up a fragile, precious relationship. She calmed the fears he had in this strange place, and he began to teach her to read and write. But the young man could not settle and decided to return to town life. The child was not told but she over-heard him talking about his intention to leave. Pain filled her heart and tears welled in her eyes. As he was leaving the village for the last time the man took some money out of his purse and called the girl in order to give it to her.

She is down at the well fetching a bucket of water, but within earshot. Carefully she wipes the tears out of her eyes. Then, body erect and head held high she walks straight past him, ignoring the voice and outstretched hand. At this point the film, one by the Indian producer Sanjayit Ray, ends, on a note of almost unbearable poignancy—a double pain, the pain of a newly formed so-much-needed relationship ended and the pain of pain enclosed, drawn tight within, and endured.

This double pain was present in many of the early poems of the Welsh poet R. S. Thomas when he wrote about a poor hill farmer struggling to make a living against the wind and the rain. In one of them he explained that he has chosen

              the story of one whose hands
Have bruised themselves on the locked doors
Of life; whose heart, fuller than mine
Of gulped tears, is the dark well
From which to draw, drop after drop,
The terrible poetry of his kind.

The dark well from which he drew the poems was a heart full of gulped tears — a person who suffered and quietly endured, who simply chose to go on going on.

A well known priest in the First World War was a man called Studdert Kennedy, nicknamed Woodbine Willy from his agreeable habit of carrying sacks of Woodbine cigarettes wherever he went. In one of his poems he tells of crawling from trench to trench giving a hasty burial service over one body after another. Then a figure loomed,

There spoke a dripping sergeant,
When the time was growing late,
'Would you please to bury this one,
'cause 'e used to be my mate?'

As the service is being said a flare goes up and the priest sees the sergeant's face set in a particular expression. The poem ends,

There are many kinds of sorrow
In this world of love and hate,
But there is no sterner sorrow
Than a soldier's for his mate.

A stern sorrow! How inadequate he must have felt before it to convey the reality of the God in whom he believed. Everything around shouted out against the idea of a love behind the universe. Yet the fact is that despite everything Studdert Kennedy did convey something of his faith to those men to whom he ministered in the trenches. Through sharing their griefs and sorrows, bearing them within himself, he conveyed something of his belief that in God also there are gulped tears and a stern sorrow. In his letter to the Galatians, Paul wrote, 'Bear one another's burdens and so fulfil the law of Christ.' This is the way, the only way, in which a softer light may come to shine in hearts set hard in resigned fortitude.

O God, we remember before you those who bravely endure.
Help us in some way to share their burden and so fulfil the law of Christ.

BLOSSOMS OF GRIEF AND CHARITY

The poet Edwin Muir wrote a lovely autobiography in which he described his idyllic childhood in the Orkney Islands, life in a Glasgow slum where most of his family died, his time on the continent when the Nazis were flexing their ugly muscles and his period in Prague after the war when the communists were taking over. At the end of this story in summing up his experiences he wrote,

> Now and then during these years I fell into the dumps for short or prolonged periods ... and passed through stretches of blankness and deprivation. From these I learned things which I could not otherwise have learned, so that I cannot regard them as mere loss. Yet I believe that I would have been better without them.

I like this passage because it is so balanced, so moderate, so truthful. He knows he has learned something from his patches of depression but in the end, and one can almost feel the quiet intensity of the words, 'I believe that I would have been better without them'.

What Edwin Muir says is important because it's very easy for people with faith—and by the end of his life he had become a Christian—to suppose that unhappiness must always serve some good purpose; to think of misfortune as sent by God to test our character. But such a view won't hold. It's true that difficulties do sometimes bring out unexpected qualities in people but we wouldn't think much of a friend who deliberately made life as uncomfortable as possible for us in order to strengthen our character—a friend who tripped us up and broke our leg in order to see how we would react in adversity is a strange kind of friend. I can't believe in a God who spends his time devising misfortunes for people, even if he does it with the best of intentions. God wishes us well.

Yet, having said that, it is an undoubted fact that when things are going badly for us we sometimes learn things we couldn't otherwise have learned. Muir mentions his dumps, his periods of depression which no one would wish on to another. Yet often it is only when we ourselves are feeling low that we begin to understand how so many others feel; it's then that we are likely to develop greater sensitivity and be less inclined to slap someone on the back with a hearty 'Cheer up, old chap' when they are feeling close to suicide. The uncomfortable fact is that many of the qualities we most admire in others have developed partly because the going has been rough. Muir himself puts this beautifully in a poem, One Foot in Eden, in which he contrasts an imagined paradise at the beginning of time with life as it is now in all its sin and sorrow. The 'famished field and blackened tree' of our experience, he says,

Bear flowers in Eden never known.
Blossoms of grief and charity
Bloom in these darkened fields alone.
What had Eden ever to say
Of hope and faith and pity and love?

In trying to assess the dark periods of our lives there is a problem that can't be solved. God did not wish such times upon us—we may have been better without them. Yet in such periods we learn to live with more sensitivity and kindness, and also more profoundly, for we begin to sense what life is really about and our previous cheery obliviousness comes to seem rather superficial. There is no neat answer to the intellectual question. But at the practical level there is I think enough light to go on. God doesn't wish us this blankness and deprivation. But it is not total loss. Some good, for others and ourselves, can be wrung from it. In the darkened field of our life will bloom blossoms of grief and charity that had not been seen before.

O God, when things seem against us and we feel depressed, show us your deeper truths, enable us to be of use to others, and bring us, with them, to that fullness of life, that peace and joy, which you will for all your children.

Through the Year

ADVENT

In Tolstoy's novel, *War and Peace*, there is a painful scene when Moscow is being evacuated. The wealthy Rostovs are piling all their goods on to carts and preparing to leave when a party of wounded soldiers arrives. Natasha, the daughter, orders the carts to be cleared of possessions so that the sick soldiers can leave too. But her mother, thinking only of her things, is furious, and countermands the order. Natasha refuses to give way and eventually the soldiers are allowed a place on the carts. It is then discovered that one of the wounded soldiers sheltering in the house is none other than Prince Andrei, the man whom Natasha loves. Natasha had ministered to a group of unknown, dirty, wounded soldiers and one of them is revealed as her beloved.

One of the themes traditionally thought about during Advent is that of judgement and in many churches the famous story in Matthew 25 will be read. Mankind is divided into two groups. The first are told, 'Come, O blessed of my father, inherit the kingdom prepared for you from the foundation of the world; for I was hungry and you gave me food, I was thirsty and you gave me drink'. The members of this group are very surprised and wonder when they did such things, and the king replies 'Truly, I say to you, as you did it to one of the least of these my brethren, you did it to me.' The same criteria of judgement is used with the other group—in so far as they failed to help someone in need, they failed to help

Christ. This story is a powerful one and it has inspired Christians in every age.

In 1527 when Breslau in Germany was hard hit by the plague Christians wondered if they ought to stay or flee. Martin Luther wrote an open letter to John Hess in which he said, 'I know very well that if Christ himself or his mother were now ill, everybody would be so devoted as to wish to help and serve ... Everybody would come running. Yet they do not want to hear what he himself says: "inasmuch as ye have done it unto one of the least of my brethren, ye have done it unto me". If then you would minister to and wait upon Christ, behold you have a sick neighbour before you. Go to him and minister to him and you will assuredly find Christ in him.'

Mother Teresa of Calcutta is another person who has been inspired by this parable. She has written, 'In holy communion we have Christ under the appearance of bread. In our work we find him under the appearance of flesh and blood. It is the same Christ. "I was hungry, I was naked, I was sick, I was homeless".' It isn't always easy to see Christ in people we don't like, even if they are in need, as Mother Teresa herself finds—but she tries 'Dearest Lord,' she prays, 'though you hide yourself behind the unattractive disguise of the irritable, the exacting, the unreasonable, may I still recognize you and say: "Jesus, my patient, how sweet it is to serve you".'

Help us good Lord, during this day, to be open and sensitive to the needs of other people and to love you in and through them.

CHRISTMAS

At Christmas 150 years ago the poet, Robert Browning, his wife and new baby were living in Florence. Like many people today he did not like the Christian churches and he was doubtful about the truth of what they preached.

In Florence there were chapels and Browning found these buildings, and those who worshipped in them, drab and dingy. He loved what was beautiful and believed God should be worshipped in beauty. He was switched off by what he considered to be the uninteresting, ragged people in the chapels, the silly sermons and the terrible noise that passed for singing. He found the chapels squalid, and he was even less drawn to the Roman Catholic Church. Whenever he thought of it he remembered the wicked popes and the long history of corruption. It seemed an all too obviously human—indeed a warped—body. Finally he doubted the truth of the Christian faith itself. It seemed incredible, unbelievable. But the learned professors who expounded it to men like himself attracted him no more than the chapels or the Roman Catholic Church. They seemed so dry. He did not think religious faith could be conveyed in such an arid way.

Three strongly negative feelings. They would only be overcome by an experience; and such an experience is what Robert Browning did have during Christmas 1849. He saw a moon-rainbow, a glorious thing, and through this glory the truth of heaven slid into his soul. He came to believe. As Owen Chadwick has written, 'He came at last to a simple answer. Whatever the philosophers might say, however others might shrink back, he at least must go and kneel at the manger. His mind still doubted. His faith knelt down. For the rest of his life his faith continued to kneel before the Christ, and thereby to inspire his poetry.' He came to believe, and although it was an experience of great beauty through which God took hold of his soul, it came with the conviction that if Christ was in beauty he was no less in the dingy chapel with its drab people; Christ was also in the soiled, worn-out lives of the poor which he had found so unattractive. Again, as Owen Chadwick has written, 'At this time Browning found an optimism about the world which was never to leave him. There is a kind of optimism which is optimistic because it is blind. Browning became an optimist but a Christian optimist; that is one who sees the world as it is, as often soiled and often criminal. Browning himself was fascinated, almost obsessed by the wickedness of the world. See the vice, and the folly, and the tawdriness, and the transitoriness and the pretence of the world—and then have hope.'

We live in serious times. Every day brings forecasts of gloom. As the old year dies away and the new looms up I expect that you will be wondering aloud with your family and friends just what it might have in store. The Christian faith suggests that hope is still the proper attitude to have. But when it says this, it does not mean that everything is going to turn out just as we want it. It means that, whatever happens, life is shot through with possibilities of loving God and man and that these possibilities are rooted in the promise of the eternal God which nothing can break or thwart. At Christmas 1849 Browning found an optimism about the world that was never to leave him. It came riding in on the carolling air. May something of this hope take hold of us too. See the vice and the folly and the tawdriness and the transitoriness and the pretence of the world—and then have hope.

Eternal God,
Your purpose will not fail,
Your promise will not be broken,
Let your hope take hold of us.

EPIPHANY

There are many different kinds of darkness. The sense of loss, for example, when someone close to us dies; the loneliness and mental depression which afflict so many, the feelings of isolation and rejection which most people experience from time to time. But there is a darkness more basic than any of these—that which comes from believing life is futile, ugly and evil, that there is no God, that men and women are simply clever animals with a flimsy covering of civilization and that when this is torn off we quickly fall below the level of the beasts.

Joseph Conrad knew this darkness. His sombre view of life is described accurately enough by Bertrand Russell when he wrote, 'Conrad thought of civilized and morally tolerable life as a dangerous walk on a thin crust of barely cooled lava which at any moment might break and let the unwary sink into fiery depths.' And nowhere does this feeling come across more strongly than in Conrad's short story, *Heart of Darkness*. In the days when European trading posts were first being set up along the rivers of central Africa a certain Mr Kurtz goes out with idealistic notions of spreading good. But something goes mysteriously and badly wrong. Just what is not too explicit, but Conrad conveys the sense that the wilderness has found Kurtz out and got him in its grip. It had whispered to him things about himself that he did not know. It had corrupted and degraded him. Finally, just before he dies Kurtz gets a glimpse of the black reality about him and within him and whispers, 'The horror, the horror.'

Conrad believed, as he put it in that story, that life is a mysterious arrangement of merciless logic for a futile purpose. And he let himself face the full implications of this black view of things. Most of us protect ourselves from the darkness by immersion in the daily routine, by distractions, by not looking too deep or too long, by clutching about ourselves a blanket of comfortable half-beliefs. Conrad did not protect himself in this way. He saw civilized and moral behaviour as the thin covering it is — and the darkness outside, encroaching.

The church believes, and proclaims during the Epiphany season, that God can bring us out of this darkness — can bring us out of darkness into his own marvellous light. Recently I saw two paintings at the National Gallery which seemed to show this so much more clearly than words are able to do. The first was a picture of the birth of Christ and the adoration of the shepherds painted in 1490 by a monk, a man who in English would be called Little Gerard of the brotherhood of St. John. He lived in Holland and died when he was only 28. He depicts the birth of Christ taking place at night, which was unusual in paintings at that time. Half of the picture is deep darkness. But in the manger the Christ child shines with luminous intensity and the brightness of this child lights up the faces of those who are gazing down, the serene devout face of Mary, others who have come to worship and even an angel in the sky. The only light is that given off by the babe and this illuminates those who have come to worship. The same point was made in painting terms by Rembrandt 150 years later. In his picture on the same theme the stable is dark; in fact most of the picture is dark. But a small group of people can be seen bending over a manger and from this the brilliant light of the Christ Child lights up their reverent faces. You may have seen this picture for it is a favourite one for Christmas cards.

To all of us at times life seems bleak and futile. But there is a purpose behind it. This purpose is not remote, cold and inhuman, but *for* us — on our side, helping us to win through. This purpose has become one with a human personality and revealed himself through a human life. Christ, who reveals God to be with us and for us, is a light shining in the darkness.

Christ, son of Mary, eternal Son of God, you have brought us out of darkness into your own marvellous light. Alleluia.

LENT

If someone says to us, 'Go on, prove you love me, buy me a car. If you buy me a car then I'll know you care for me,' we resent them. We sniff emotional blackmail in the air and instinctively we feel that such behaviour is out of place between people who say they care for one another. You have to let people show their love in their own way at their own time. You don't try to force them. You trust them. What is true here is even more true in our relationship with God. People are sometimes tempted to make God show his hand. 'If you're really there, God, prove it. If Betty gets better then I'll believe in you'. Now it may be that you and I have never been tempted to think like that; but it could be that such temptations only come to those who care desperately enough about God. To Christ for example. Christ was tested much more severely, not less, than we are.

Take just one of the famous three temptations in the wilderness. At his baptism Christ had heard the words, 'Thou art my beloved Son—with thee I am well-pleased'. The temptations concern the way in which he is to interpret and live out this sonship. They all begin, 'If you are the Son of God'. Why the 'if' unless there was some doubt in his own mind? If so, it was perfectly natural. Who wouldn't doubt a conviction that he had been called to live as a divine Son? 'Is it really God calling me or just my unconscious? Am I deluding myself?' So Christ is tempted to get definite proof that he really is the Son of God—not so much for others as for himself. In his mind's eye he sees himself standing on the parapet surrounding the great temple in Jerusalem looking down 450 feet below into the Kedron valley. 'Throw yourself down. If you really are the Son of God, God will make sure you don't hurt yourself. Don't you dare? If you want God to show his power you must be prepared to take a risk too. Doesn't it say in Psalm 91 that he will protect you come what may. 'He will give his angels orders to take care of you. They will support you in their arms for fear you should strike your foot against a stone.'

But Christ recognizes this voice for the insidious temptation it is and remembers the words from Deuteronomy—'You are not to test the Lord your God'. Trying to force God to prove his love is utterly inappropriate. We are not to test him but to trust him. So it was that with much struggle and anguish—I don't for one moment think the temptations were confined to 40 days in the wilderness—Christ pioneered for us the way of trust. Through rejection, betrayal, desertion, pain of body, mocking, humiliation, apparent total failure, there was an underlying, absolute trust. He opened up a route for us to follow: trust—whatever our circumstances.

You taught us Lord that behind our lives is a faithful one, the Father, and you lived out your life in faith to the bitter end.
Deepen our trust and bless those who are having a rough time, for you now live and reign with the Father and the Holy Spirit, one God, world without end.

HOLY WEEK

Waiting for Godot is one of the most famous of modern plays. In it four tramp-like figures are depicted waiting; waiting for they know not quite what. Near the beginning Vladimir starts up a somewhat surprising subject. 'Two thieves', he says, 'crucified at the same time as our Saviour.' Estragon is puzzled. 'Our what?' he says. 'Our Saviour', Vladimir replies. 'Two thieves. One is supposed to have been saved and the other . . . damned.' Vladimir, it emerges, is troubled because of the four gospels only one speaks of a thief being saved. Estragon can't see what the fuss is about. But Vladimir is concerned and disturbed. 'But all four were there. And only one speaks of a thief being saved. Why believe him rather than the others?' It matters to him that there is a Saviour; a Saviour of criminals.

As a preparation for Holy Week I would like to think a little more about that enigmatic, haunting figure who was crucified beside Christ. The other thief, if you remember, joined in the taunts of the crowd, bitterly reproaching Jesus. 'Are you not the Christ? Save yourself and us.' He tries to relieve a little of his own desperate hurt by taking it out on someone weaker than himself. The other thief objects. There is a certain kind of person, to be met the world over, who is rough, even violent but who at bottom has a certain simple sense of right and wrong. When they do wrong and are punished for it know that this is not the worst thing that can happen to them. One of the robbers appears to have been a person like that. He senses something of Christ's innocence. He has a basic sense of fair play and an awareness that there is something more final than a human court of judgement. He blurts out, 'Do you not fear God, since you are under the same sentence of condemnation? And we indeed justly; for we are receiving the due reward of our deeds; but this man has done nothing wrong.' He then turns to Christ and says, 'Jesus, remember me when you come in your kingly power.' People have sometimes wondered if the thief really could have believed Jesus to be the Messiah about to come into his own; was he perhaps just trying to humour Jesus out of pity? But I rather like the line of thought in a poem by the modern Argentinian poet Borges which suggests that the very simplicity which made him ask for and be granted paradise was what drove him time and again to sin and to bloody crime. A man who even in crime had a kind of directness. Whatever the reason, he turned to Christ with the same directness and made the most enormous request. And Christ granted it. 'Truly, I say to you, today you will be with me in paradise.'

To Luke, who records this scene, and to the first Christians, this story had a powerful fascination. A great number of those first followers would have been slaves, or from the roughest, poorest element in society—not at all respectable people. The letters in the New Testament are always warning against such unsophisticated sins as thieving and drunkenness. But there it is. A crucified criminal can recognize Christ. To a dying desperado, the word of God's grace can come. This almost unspeakably moving and impressive story seems to strip away the layers of pretence with which our lives are normally clothed. It confronts us with the rough, raw reality of human existence. It's a hopeless case, a punished, rejected dying write-off, who recognizes Christ. To him Christ promises everything. It's never too late, says the story. Between the stirrup and the ground as the old saying put it. No one, but no one, is so degraded, that they cannot hear the promise of his love which God makes to each human soul.

Grant us, O God, to recognize you and to hear the word you speak to us.

GOOD FRIDAY

If someone got you in a corner and winkled out of you what you really thought of other people, I wonder what you would say. I think I'd want to say that whilst there are one or two right B's around most of us are ordinary reasonably decent people and in this category I would place myself. Then something comes along which raises a question mark against this benign view — like Good Friday. For it was human beings who tortured to death the Son of God, the most perfect person who has ever lived. It forces me to rethink. What seems to be wrong with my view of human nature is the supposition that the harm done in the world is brought about by a few wicked men who consciously set out to do wrong. But this just isn't true. We are moral beings, and one of the disturbing aspects of this is that when we do wrong we nearly always justify what we do not just to others, but to ourselves, in moral terms. Even when people are bringing about destruction on a massive scale they kid themselves that they are doing right.

I was brought up in the Second World War to believe that Goebbels, like the other Nazis, was an evil man. Recently a Sunday newspaper has been serializing his diaries. What do they reveal? A man brooding in darkness plotting deeds of horror? On the contrary he is full of moral indignation against what he calls the great gangster Churchill and says he ought to be dealing with all the strikes in England instead of digging Germany's grave. At one point he writes, 'It should be our ambition to ensure that should a similar great crisis arise in Germany, say in 150 years time, our grandchildren may look back on us as a heroic example of steadfastness.' On the whole we don't deliberately set out to do evil. The problem is that we are blind and we keep ourselves blind. We deceive ourselves. 'Father, forgive them, for they know not what they do,' prayed Christ. I can just imagine Pilate justifying the crucifixion in terms of law and order. The religious leaders talking about the importance of preserving a God-given revelation from heretical upstarts. The crowd saying, 'What's it got to do with us anyway?' The cross leads us to question all easy complacent understandings of ourselves. It probes and unsettles our self-image.

Not long ago the National Theatre staged a production of the York mystery play on the Passion. After Christ had been placed on a huge cross and hoisted up, from where he dominated the stage, the actors changed out of their Roman armour into work clothes. For it was a kind of play in a play. They were representing medieval workers putting on a play. One player put on overalls and a miner's helmet with a lamp in it. He stood at the foot of the cross and looked up so that the beam lit up the face of Christ. Then he turned slowly round the audience. The beam of light cut through the darkness of the theatre, and seemed to cut through the heart of everyone there. The cross of Christ is a light that penetrates the heart, searching, probing the springs of action.

Almighty God, we beseech thee graciously to behold this thy family, for which our Lord Jesus Christ was contented to be betrayed, and given up into the hands of wicked men, and to suffer death upon the cross, who now liveth and reigneth with thee and the Holy Spirit, ever one God world without end. Amen.

EASTER

Like many fathers of young boys I was badgered to take my son to the film *Star Wars*. It's not, frankly, my scene. I have nothing against science fiction as such; it's just that I find what goes on in people infinitely more interesting than what goes on in outer space. But obviously I had to go, though predictably, after a few minutes I was fast asleep. However, after a short nap I woke up and enjoyed the excellent simulation of space ships moving around and attacking one another. The plot, like all adventure stories, concerns a struggle between a group of good people and a group of evil ones though the special factor about this story is that the goodies have what they call 'The Force' on their side. The Force is a spiritual power behind, beyond and within things which helps them in time of trouble; and it is personified in a wise old chap called by the unlikely name of Ben obi wan Kenobi. In the course of the fighting Ben Kenobi is killed, though not before he has told his companions and successors in the fight, 'The Force will be with you—always'. Ben Kenobi is killed but after his death his body is suddenly no longer there. His clothes remain but there is no corpse. It vanishes into thin air, and after this whenever Luke Skywalker, the hero, and his friends are in trouble they seem to hear the voice of Ben Kenobi guiding and protecting them.

Now I don't want to make out that this film is a profoundly religious experience. It's not that kind of film. But it's obvious from what I have mentioned that there are meant to be parallels with the first Easter. Christ too taught that behind, beyond and within things there is a spiritual power, though he called this power 'Abba, Father', not 'The Force'. Men came to see in him a personification, a revelation in human terms, of this power. And after his death—the Gospels report that his body could not be found, only the grave clothes remained—the disciples believed he was with them still, guiding them and inspiring them to carry on his work.

I don't think there is any very deep reason why the makers of this film make such allusions. In a way it is natural enough. There is a great interest in religion these days and America is a country where the Christian faith is still very strong. But having said that the film might help some people understand a little more the mystery of that first Easter. Those early Christians believed that at his death Jesus had kind of melted into God—or to put it another way, that the essential being of Jesus, as Son of God, was revealed as always having been one with the Father. Death did not destroy. It simply showed what the disciples had dimly begun to realize, that the being of Jesus was, and always had been, grounded in God. So it was that they had no hesitation about praying to Christ as easily as they had always prayed to God. They could no longer think of God without thinking of Jesus in whom he had revealed his heart and mind of love. They were conscious of his guidance and his strengthening as they tried to carry on his work. This was their experience. It was this that launched the Christian church in the first place and it is this which is at the heart of its life today.

We praise you, O Christ, that neither human rejection, cruel fate, nor even death could separate you from the Father, and that in you nothing can separate us from his love either.

WHITSUN

One of the most puzzling aspects of human life is the strange sense of dissatisfaction which we human beings seem to share. I don't mean the sense of frustration that comes when things go wrong with our lives—when we don't get the job or girl-friend we want—that's understandable enough. Nor do I mean the dissatisfaction whose roots are psychological. What I am referring to can come when things are going well and although it is a sense of dissatisfaction, it is not altogether a disagreeable feeling. It often comes through experiences of beauty. On the way to church in the mornings I am lucky enough to pass some lilac. I can rarely resist breathing in some of its fragrance. It is utterly satisfying and yet can at the same time leave a yearning for something beyond itself. Beauty evokes strange nameless longings for something more than the immediate experience. Wordsworth once wrote,

Not in entire forgetfulness,
And not in utter nakedness,
But trailing clouds of glory do we come
From God, who is our home:
Heaven lies about us in our infancy!
Shades of the prison-house begin to close
Upon the growing boy,
But he beholds the light, and whence it flows,
He sees it in his joy;
Intimations of Immortality from Recollections of Early Childhood.

Behind these lines there lies the sense of an environment of glory which is our true home but one from which we are mostly cut off.

Another passage speaks even more directly of this experience. The writer, J. W. N. Sullivan, recalls a moment of childhood. 'I remember vividly my first experience of the kind when, as a boy, I came suddenly upon the quiet miracle of an ivy-clad wall glistening under a London street-lamp. I wanted to weep and I wanted to pray; to weep for the paradise from which I had been exiled, and to pray that I might yet be made worthy of it.'

And underlying the stories in the book of Genesis there seems to be the same experience. Adam and Eve are conscious of being exiled from a garden of paradise. I don't take this as a literal account of what happened to some first human beings, but the story does reflect a universal human experience, something which human beings everywhere have experienced. On the one hand we are conscious of a glory, a paradise to which we rightly belong. On the other hand we know ourselves to be in some way cut off, estranged from it.

Whit Sunday is the feast of the Holy Spirit. It is the day in the year when the church remembers the great unleashing of divine Spirit into human life after the death, resurrection and ascension of Christ. Using picture language — the only language we have got — the Holy Spirit is the bond of love between God the Father and God the Son. This love, this Spirit, overflows from the fullness of the Godhead into human life. Cardinal Newman once wrote, 'Christ came to make a new world . . . to make a new beginning.' And that's just what the first Christians felt had happened. They had a marvellous feeling of life starting all over again. They were filled with a sense of marvel and wonder. They wanted to praise. They wanted to share all their possessions with other people. They must have felt it was the first day of creation in the garden of Eden all over again.

Whoever we are, whether we regard ourselves as religious or not, the Holy Spirit is active in our lives. Those strange longings that come through experiences of beauty are the work of the Spirit. So also are those moments when we feel at one with God or another person. And there can be much more of this sense of walking in paradise on the first day of creation if we are prepared to live consciously in harmony with God's spirit in our hearts.

O God, Holy Spirit, active in our lives, make all things new.

TRINITY

The English on the whole have been a practical people; less interested in the finer points of religious doctrine than what good will result from them. Jonathan Swift, Dean of St. Patrick's Cathedral, Dublin, in the 18th century, the author of *Gulliver's Travels*, and one of the most interesting people ever born, once wrote, 'Men should consider that raising difficulties concerning the mysteries of religion cannot make them more wise, learned or virtuous; better neighbours or friends.' What a splendid douche of cold water that is just before Trinity Sunday when the church rejoices in the fact of God as Father, Son and Holy Spirit and inevitable questions come into the mind. Today we are aware not only of Jonathan Swift's point—will our religious ponderings make us better people—but of the difficulty of talking about God in human terms at all.

Philip Toynbee has written,

> 'To many of us who are deeply concerned with religious truth the whole concept of making it a subject for disputation seems wrong to the point of blasphemy. We believe that formal creeds and

dogmas are at best a sort of metaphorical stutter; that the Spirit may be known through love, through prayer and through right action but that this knowledge can never be formulated in the language of human debate. We do much better', he added, 'to praise God together than to argue about which set of defining words is the less grotesquely inadequate and misleading.'

When I first read this, I wanted to shout 'Hear, Hear' — at best our talk about God is a metaphorical stutter.

But, having said this, we still want to ask, I think, why should we believe that God is Holy Trinity, three persons in one God. I know how the belief arose. God first revealed himself to be the faithful Father, maker of heaven and earth; then Jesus lived out his life as a Son in relation to this Father, and the resurrection revealed this Father/Son relationship to be an eternal fact. Then, after the death of Jesus, his followers experienced his continuing presence as a loving power within them and in their community life. And I know that the church after many centuries of thinking about it believed that this wasn't just God expressing himself in three different ways but that he is eternally, in himself, Father, Son and Holy Spirit. I know this — but why should I believe it to be true? The best answer I've heard is that given by Austin Farrer who pointed out that mind is a social reality. What he meant was that there can be no such thing as a completely solitary individual. Even the hermit in the desert was once formed as a person through his relationship with his parents and other people. Because others talked to him he began to talk and think. And in the desert he still relates to others through thought and prayer. Mind is always mind in relationship to other minds. So when we think of God as personal or infinite mind we are to think of loving relationship as somehow contained within the Godhead. And that's perhaps as far as we can go.

But let me come down to earth again. For God is not a pile of words to be strung in the right order. He is a spiritual reality who can be known, as Philip Toynbee said, 'only through love, through prayer and through right action'. A friend of mine went into hospital not long ago to have a baby. Sadly she lost the baby but she wrote in a letter afterwards, 'All through the long night of delivery I had a very vivid experience of the Trinity, in that I felt secure in the care of the Father, comforted by the Spirit and empathetic with the sufferings of the Son . . . I felt so close to God all during that time.' Perhaps this girl had a very special experience. But what she talked about is open to all of us. God is at one and the same time the trustworthy Father on whom we can utterly depend. He is not cold and detached but in his Son knows the pain of our lives at first hand and shares our personal struggle with us. Though always beyond us as the one to whom we can relate, he is also present in the deepest core of our being as a Spirit giving us a strength beyond our normal human resources.

May God, Father, Son and Holy Spirit, bless us now and always.

Peace and Joy

ARE YOU HAPPY?

I was once sitting next to an acquaintance, talking about this and that, when suddenly she leant over, looked at me intensely and said, 'Are you happy?' I was startled and somewhat embarrassed. For the subject of our own happiness, like death and sex, is not one on which we find it easy to lay bare our inmost feelings. The person who shot this question was herself somewhat discontented and restless; and she had the feeling that others possessed a happiness which she was missing out on. And there are many people like her today, who are not happy but who feel they could and ought to be. In this respect we are very different from those who lived even a hundred years ago. Then people expected life to be made up of much toil and pain. Look at all those Victorian hymns. They are full of phrases like 'through the night of doubt and sorrow' and 'Lead kindly light amid the encircling gloom'. And these hymns bring out another crucial difference between our grandparents and ourselves. They had for the most part a mental framework, a view of life, in which the pain of life could be understood and made bearable. They thought of life as a hard and difficult journey to a better country; or as Keats put it 'a vale of soul making'. And if you know you are on the road to somewhere worth going, you are prepared to do a bit of roughing it on the way.

Who is right, I wonder, the Victorians who resigned themselves to life as a long uphill struggle or ourselves who expect to be happy? In some respects undoubtedly, we are. Our forebears were prone to resign themselves too easily to misery which could have been eliminated — particularly when it was other people's. Many hardships they put up with have now been done away and there is much human travail that can and must eventually be reduced. Yet, finally, our hope that life will give us an easy care-free happiness is an illusion.

First, there is a hard core of mental pain that will always be with us — the general insecurity of life and our proneness to accident, the prospect of death, grief and the sheer difficulty of making relationships with other less than perfect people like ourselves. Of course there are moments and even long periods of happiness — times when things go well with us and we feel good, when as in the song of the old musical we want to skip and sing, 'Just singing in the rain, I'm happy again'. For such moments which cannot be manufactured we can only be deeply grateful. But these apart there is enough anguish around to make us agree with the 17th century doctor, Sir Thomas Browne, that 'Certainly there is no happiness within this circle of flesh'. Second, and even more important, those who have made the greatest contribution to human life — great writers, poets, artists, musicians, saints — have almost always not been what we would call happy. Often they have been deeply troubled people — people who have agonized to grasp the truth of things at deeper and deeper levels. They have acted on the belief of the philosopher John Stuart Mill that 'It is better to be a human being dissatisfied than a pig satisfied, better to be Socrates dissatisfied than a fool satisfied.'

Life then does not offer an easy trouble-free path to happiness, and most crucial of all, those whom we most admire have almost always regarded other values as more important. Instead of happiness the Christian faith offers something else. Anthony Bloom once said, 'If you are really aware of things, of how tragic life is, then there is restraint in your enjoyment ... enjoying the outer aspect of life with the awareness of so many people suffering is something which I find difficult.' But he went on to say, 'Joy is another thing. One can possess a great sense of inner joy and elation.' How do we attain to this profound enduring quality he called joy? Perhaps I may leave it as a question in the mind.

O God, our Heavenly Father, we long for happiness; but lead us beyond happiness to a joy from which nothing can take away, through Jesus Christ our Lord.

THE TENDER SMILE

I think everyone will be familiar with the words which Jesus quoted from the Old Testament to sum up the first and most important duty of mankind: 'Love the Lord your God with all your heart, with all your soul, with all your mind and with all your strength.' But what does this actually mean? There is an obvious sense in which we can love God by trying to please him. And Christ has told us quite clearly what does please God. 'This is my commandment to you', says the Jesus of John's gospel; 'love one another.' The epistle of John puts it even more sharply: 'If a person doesn't love the brother whom he's seen it cannot be that he loves God whom he hasn't seen.' But loving someone means more than trying to please them however basic this might be. We want to be with them, to enjoy their company. But how can we be with God to enjoy his company? It's an idea many find strange and difficult. Yet, there have been Christians for whom it has been utterly real.

The great Spanish mystics of the 16th century, St. John of the Cross and St. Teresa, loved God more passionately than Romeo loved Juliet or Juliet Romeo. St. Teresa's poems are full of such phrases as 'Sweetest spouse, my life thou art' and 'Sweetest love I come to Thee.' Yet here again I suppose we moderns will want to raise a question. Teresa was a nun, John of the Cross a monk. When they wrote love poems to God full of such passionate tenderness wasn't this just a displaced or sublimated form of human love? To put it bluntly, if they had been married with normal sex lives would they still have written such poems to God? I believe they would, because even the richest human experiences leave a sense that there is something more.

C. S. Lewis married rather late in life. Later he wrote,

> 'One thing marriage has done for me. I can never again believe that religion is manufactured out of our unconscious, starved desires and is a substitute for sex. For those few years H and I feasted on love; every mode of it . . . No cranny of heart or body remained unsatisfied. If God were a substitute for love we ought to have lost all interest in him . . . but that isn't what happens. We both knew we wanted something besides one another—quite a different kind of something, a quite different kind of want.'

Some people are strongly aware of this longing for something more in experiences of beauty. Beauty both satisfies and leaves us restless for something beyond itself. As Simone Weil once put it, writing of something beautiful, 'We do not desire anything else, we possess it, and yet we still desire something. We do not in the least know what it is. We want to get behind beauty but it is only a surface. It is a sphinx, an enigma, a mystery which is painfully tantalising.'

But one great practical difficulty arises. How can we love what we don't see and can't imagine? For most there is only one way. We have to love the eternal as it makes itself known in and through the temporal. Take the flowers that come out with such colourful exuberance. Do we find them glorious? Their glory is only the humblest thread in the coat of divine glory. Kneeling alone in a room do we find a stillness and peace? It is but a whisper from the endless forests of divine stillness. If there is beauty, peace, love to be found in this world, how much more, oh how much more, is it to be found in God. And what we love in the world about us not only points beyond itself, but it bodies forth and conveys what is beyond to us. In the love of others divine love breaks through; in the beauty of the world, divine beauty can be glimpsed. As Simone Weil put it, 'The beauty of the world is Christ's tender smile for us coming through matter.' If we can find anything to love in this world we can begin to love the God who meets us in and through what we love.

O God, we find it strange and difficult to love you, but help us to love this world and especially the people in it, and grant that we may come to meet and love you in and through what we love.

RESTLESS FOR GOD

When you think of the people to whom you are closest, what, I wonder, do you really want for them? Happiness, yes, but what are the ingredients of happiness? Most of us would say, someone to love and be loved by, and a satisfying job. But even given these really good gifts, would we be satisfied? George Herbert wrote a poem, *The Pulley*, in which he pictures God making man and pouring upon him every blessing—except one.

When God at first made man,
Having a glasse of blessings standing by;
Let us (said he) poure on him all we can:
Let the worlds riches, which dispersed lie,
    Contract into a span.

So strength first made a way;
Then beautie flow'd, then wisdome, honour, pleasure:
When almost all was out, God made a stay,
Perceiving that alone of all his treasure
    Rest in the bottome lay.

According to Herbert's poem God withheld from man one blessing—rest, or peace of heart.

Living at the time we do our natural inclination is to suggest that our human restlessness has a psychological origin; to say it is the sign of some inner frustration which could be put right. Perhaps it is for some people, but as the passage quoted in the last meditation makes clear, C. S. Lewis and his wife both discovered that they wanted something besides one another.

Even when we have all the ingredients of human happiness there is another kind of want, which Herbert thinks of as deliberately left in us by God so that we won't rest content in the good things of this life but will reach beyond them to God himself. Thinking of this rest or peace of heart he goes on,

For if I should (said he)
Bestow this jewell also on my creature,
He would adore my gifts instead of me,
and rest in Nature, not the God of Nature
        So both should losers be.

Yet let him keep the rest,
But keep them with repining restlessness:
Let him be rich and wearie, that at least,
If goodnesse leade him not, yet wearinesse
        May tosse him to my breast.

We have been created with a repining restlessness,
with a homing instinct for God. As Augustine put it in the
opening paragraph of his *Confessions*, 'You have made
us for yourself and our hearts are restless until they rest
in you.' That is a famous, lovely phrase but in all honesty
not one that most of us could pray very ardently. Oh yes,
we are conscious, more than conscious, of the frustra-
tions of daily life, of longings for all sorts of things, but a
longing for God? That sounds a bit beyond most of us.
But perhaps we could get as far as saying, 'I want to want
you God.'

Michael Ramsey, former Archbishop of Canterbury,
said that he once got in rather a bad state so that all he
could pray was, 'I want to want to want to want you
God', but that he felt it was a real prayer because it was
sincere. He also suggested that some of the phrases in
the psalms are useful because they often express a deep
heart-longing for God which can lift our own feeble
aspirations beyond themselves. So I'm going to take up
that suggestion by using some words from Psalm 42,

Like as the hart desireth the water-brooks,
    so longeth my soul after thee O God.
My soul is athirst for God,
    yea, even for the living God.

AFFIRMING LIFE

The great benefit which people look for from a religious faith is peace of mind. This includes being at one with life itself. Being at one with life doesn't mean an easy acceptance of everything as it is. On the contrary there is much that we ought to be opposing and struggling against—physical starvation in the developing countries, emotional and spiritual starvation in the industrialized countries. But, having said that, there are in most people's lives things which just cannot be changed—the fact that someone close to us has died, or advancing old age, to take just the two obvious examples. Often the only choice open to us is between two attitudes, one of bitterness against life and the other of reconciliation to its often harsh conditions. We need that marvellous prayer of Reinhold Niebuhr, 'Grant us the courage to change what should be changed, patience to accept what cannot be changed and wisdom to discern the one from the other.'

There are certain things that just cannot be altered but we may still wonder whether acceptance is the proper response to them. From time to time we meet someone who has suffered so many misfortunes that life really does seem to be against them. Often they feel angry with fate or God and it is difficult not to sympathize with them. At the beginning of the funeral service the minister reads out some sentences from Scripture one of which goes, 'The Lord gave and the Lord hath taken away. Blessed be the name of the Lord'. I can never read it without mixed feelings. On the one hand it expresses so perfectly and positively an acceptance of the conditions under which we live our lives. On the other hand what is right for an 80 year old at the end of a full life is on other occasions so desperately inappropriate.

Ivan Karamazov in Dostoevsky's novel says that he could never love a scheme of things in which children suffer. The same note of anger comes out in the novels of Camus. At the end of *Outsider* the prison chaplain goes to visit the central character, who has been condemned to death. The prisoner lets out a great spate of rage against the heavens. This feeling in Dostoevsky and Camus is not simulated. It is a profoundly sensitive and moral response to some of the facts of human life. How then can we talk about being at one with life? Two things help I think.

First, the fact that some people who have been through great trials still manage to affirm life. In Rose Macauley's novel *The Towers of Trebizond* someone greatly loved is killed in a car crash (a situation which apparently reflected Rose Macauley's own life), and the narrator muses at the end, 'Life, for all its agonies of despair and loss and guilt is exciting and beautiful, amusing and artful and endearing, full of liking and love, at times a poem and a high adventure, at times noble and at times very gay; and whatever (if anything) is to come after it, we shall not have this life again.' An Anglican missionary society, the U.S.P.G. once published a poster showing a family in a very small kitchen. A child is looking out of the window. The mother is holding a baby. The very ordinary room is filled with loving warmth and underneath are written words from the *Desiderata*, 'With all its sham, drudgery and broken dreams, it is still a beautiful world.'

Second, people are able to make something of their lives even in the most limited and constricting of circumstances. Jesus was not brought up in Athens or tutored by a Greek philosopher, he was brought up in the home of a craftsman. He did not live at a time when his message could go straight into the homes of millions. His followers were very ordinary people as the world judges these things. He could not get people to respond to what he said. He died young after a ministry of only three years, executed on trumped up charges. But he made his life a sign of God.

Grant, O God, that however hard or limiting our circumstances we may this day discern something which enables us both to affirm life and make something of our lives, through Jesus Christ our Lord.

PASTURES STILL

A group of people from London visiting the countryside were once asked if great longings to live in a country cottage ever swept over them. All immediately replied, 'Yes.' I suspect that they, like many others, respond to Yeats' poem about the *Lake Isle of Innisfree*, in which he talks of building a small cabin by the lake with rows of beans and a hive of bees. 'And I shall have some peace there,' he says, 'for peace comes dropping slow.'

Funnily enough there are some people who can't stand the silence of the countryside. They get unnerved at night by the quiet. If you live in a town long enough the continuous noise, movement and light become a familiar and comforting surround. Sometimes if we cut out external noise we hear too clearly the shriek of inner brakes. So it's not just silence we want. It's stillness, inner peace. Silence is useful only if it leads to this. We read in the gospels that Christ used to go into the hills or the desert to be alone. Monks and nuns have regular periods of silence built into their routine. This is for a purpose. Hopkins wrote,

Elected silence sing to me
and beat upon my whorled ear.
Pipe me to pastures still
and be the music that I long to hear.

He wanted silence to lead him to stillness.

When you think of peace and quiet I wonder what scenes you think of? Perhaps a walk through a wood. All sound cut out except that of birds in the trees and stirring in the undergrowth, not even able to hear your own footsteps because of the carpet of pineneedles. Or sometimes I think of small and whitewashed rooms; of a simple, unadorned cell in a monastery or house, where people have knelt for over 1,000 years. We all have our special places.

But this isn't meant to be a nostalgic yearning for the unattainable. Most of us will have to live this day in a town, with people and noise, pressure and strain. This is where we are and to have the day punctuated by great longings to arise and go to Innisfree is not very helpful. But perhaps these longings are a projection? Perhaps we focus on something outside what in fact we want within. So I would like to end with some words that St. Francis used to give his disciples as he sent them out: 'Wherever we are, or wherever we go, we always take our cell with us; for our brother body is our cell, and our soul is the hermit who lives in it, constantly praying to God and meditating on him. If the soul cannot remain quiet in its cell, then a cell made with hands is of little value.'

Give to us good Lord, amid the pressures of this day, tranquility of spirit.

HELD IN BEING

We all want peace of mind; the serenity and inner repose that come from being at one with our fellow human beings, with ourselves, with life itself and with God. 'All that matters', wrote D. H. Lawrence, 'is to be at one with the living God, to be a creature in the house of the God of life.' Now I want to be a bit more practical and think about how we can actually go about achieving this oneness.

I begin with a thought of C. S. Lewis that I often find helpful. He knew that prayer should begin with what the prayer guides call 'putting ourselves in the presence of God' but like the rest of us was uncertain what he was actually meant to do. So he decided to begin by thinking about what was real for him, what he could see and touch; for example, the walls of the room he was in. 'The walls they say are matter', he wrote, 'that is, the physicists will try to tell me, something totally unimaginable, only mathematically describable, existing in a curved space, charged with appalling energies. If I could penetrate far enough into that mystery I should perhaps finally reach what is sheerly real.' He then asked himself the question, 'What is this thinking self, this "I" looking at these walls?' and suggested that if we dived deeply enough once again we would come up against that which simply is. So that 'either mystery, the mystery of matter and the mystery of the human self', he wrote, 'if I could follow it far enough, would lead me to the same point—the point where something, in each case unimaginable, leaps from God's naked hand.' In short, at the bottom of matter and the bottom of ourselves is the creative mystery from which all things spring forth.

Now at the risk of sounding like a poor imitation of Eileen Fowler the kind of act of imagination made by C. S. Lewis can, I think, be linked to the simple physical act of standing. During each day most of us have periods of standing with nothing very much useful to do.

Standing waiting for a bus or tube, standing in a shop waiting to pay for the groceries, waiting in a launderette, standing between jobs at the factory bench and so on. These periods of standing can be turned into moments of peace. First, by becoming conscious of ourselves as standing; letting one's weight sink down the body through the legs into the feet and becoming aware of the ground beneath supporting us. This ground, as it were holding us up, is matter; matter charged with appalling energies, and at the heart of these energies is the creative source from which all things spring forth. So the physical act of standing is linked with a movement of the imagination, and this leads naturally into a simple prayer such as, 'O God you uphold me.' One I like goes, 'God, you are the source and ground of all that is, moment by moment you hold me in being.' This can be said a number of times, with the mind held in a state of quiet stillness during the moments between. All this is quite possible even when surrounded by roar of traffic, squeals of brakes, chattering and cheerful frantic hubbub that makes up our city life.

This does not take any time. It is simply using time that would otherwise be wasted to good purpose. Most people find it difficult if not impossible to pray because as soon as they try to concentrate distractions, crowd in on the mind. What I am suggesting is that first of all we simply become aware of ourselves as a physical being, standing. In this way the whole body becomes part of the prayer, aiding the mind in its concentration. Further, this kind of prayer gets away from what someone called worrying before God. By taking some short phrase and repeating it slowly at intervals, using both the words and the silence between the words as a focus, we discover a quieter, more God-centred way of relating to the eternal. It's very simple but it works.

O God, you are the source and ground of all that is. Moment by moment you hold us in being.

BECOMING STILL

In one of his poems T. S. Eliot has a couple of rather strange little lines. They go: 'Teach us to care, and not to care, Teach us to sit still.' They express, it seems to me, a desire to live from some deeper centre of our being, a point of inner repose and stillness; and they suggest that this enables us both to care more for other people and to be free of personal anxieties and preoccupations.

A few years ago I came across these lines of Kahil Gibran: 'When God threw me a pebble into this wondrous lake I disturbed its surface with countless circles. But when I reached the depths I became very still. 'The same thought is put another way by Tagore. 'Sit still my heart, do not raise your dust. Let the world find its way to you.' These and many other teachers hold out the ideal of inner stillness. But I suppose the practical question for most people, busy in factories and offices all day and then caught up with a host of things at home, is how they can find time to achieve this stillness, and how they actually go about it.

I have already suggested that the simple act of standing can be turned into an act of trustful dependence on God the source and ground of all that exists, who moment by moment holds us in being. Now I want to indicate another way in which the ordinary moments of the day can be turned into a prayer. Most people have a few moments in the day with nothing in particular to do. Sitting in a bus or train on the way to work, sitting in the office between letters, sitting at a machine in a factory. Not much time, but a few moments and that is all that is necessary. It is helpful at such times to have in mind what I would call an image of stillness. Perhaps on a holiday you have seen a lake when the wind has dropped, trees standing quietly at the edge; the sea in the evening, beach deserted, hardly a ripple on the water. One of the glories of London is the plane trees which have a marvellous capacity to survive the fumes and dirt. In winter when the leaves have dropped and the bare branches stand out against the sky with the fruit hanging down at the end of slender stalks, they have the stillness of a Chinese painting. It could indeed be a picture that you think of—a famous painting often reproduced is Vermeer's *The Cook*. It shows a Dutch housewife pouring milk out of a jug. An ordered tranquility imbues her action and fills the room. And this reminds us that the only kind of stillness worth having is one that pervades our movements. It isn't the opposite of doing things but a quality that permeates our doing. Then there are the images from the Bible. Christ on the Lake of Galilee when a storm blew up. The disciples got in a panic but he slept quietly on, eventually saying to the fierce wind and rough sea 'Peace be still', and, as the narrative puts it, 'There was a great calm.' Even if you don't believe the story to be literally true it can be used, for the point is that Christ was a person before whom everything seemed to become still.

These are just some images of stillness. Everyone will have their own favourite ones. In an odd moment during the day the image can be brought to mind and a short line from a prayer or psalm said. Some people use the line, 'Be still and know that I am God,' said several times slowly with a pause for silence in between. In this way the mind becomes receptive to God's stillness which can break through to us. In this way we can find a deeper level of inward quiet which will imbue the next thing we have to get up and do.

O God, teach us to care, and not to care,
Teach us to sit still,
To be still and know your presence.

CAREFREE DELIGHT

Like most people I know little about modern art and much of it I find hard to understand. But someone once sent me a postcard by an artist called Paul Klee which was so full of fun, exuberance and humour that ever since I have wanted to have a good look at his paintings. When I had a chance I wasn't disappointed. The best of the pictures had a quality of sheer delight about them. The colours, and in particular the lines, had a sense of *joie de vivre*, playfulness and wit. It was as though the artist had looked at the world around him and seen a rich profusion of shapes, colours and lines all ready to dance a jig. I came away better for having seen these pictures, but wondering why most of us adults find it so difficult to achieve such carefree delight. Children often have this quality, but as Wordsworth put it, 'Shades of the prison-house begin to close upon the growing boy'. He uses a strong image, prison-house, but not I think an exaggerated one when we think of the worries that weigh so heavily on most minds.

Many of our worries are very understandable. Illness in those we love, times of strain in our relationships, things not going well in the work that means a lot to us — all this apart from the general state of present day society. Life is a serious business. Yet, on the Christian view of things, our moments of carefree delight point to a profounder truth. For God's creation of the world was not a glum-faced business. It was and is an act of joyous, loving exuberance. And in the end, when God will be all in all, every motion will have the character of carefree play. In the end as Martin Luther put it, men will play 'with heaven and earth, the sun and all creatures. All creatures shall have their fun, love and joy, and shall laugh with thee and thou with them.' For much of the time life is pretty tough going. It is very much what Keats said it was, 'a vale of soul-making'. But our moments of sheer fun and joyous abandon are a pointer to the final truth about things. They aren't just a way of escaping from the daily drudge. For through them we participate in the creative zest of God and have a foretaste of what finally will be.

But a big practical question remains. How can we find and keep this outlook amidst the pressures of modern living? There is I think no technique that can guarantee it. For these moments of delight are the result of the Holy Spirit in our life. They break into our day unexpectedly. But they do happen. Our self-preoccupation, our resentment about the past and anxieties about the future drop away and we know what Paul meant when he talked about 'the glorious liberty of the children of God'. And these moments aren't always especially religious moments. The other night I was at a party. You would have said that most of those present were getting on a bit. It wasn't swinging. We didn't even have a disco. In the end all fifty or so of us ended up playing a hilarious game of musical chairs. It was quite simply, fun; nothing pretentious. But there was release, affection, laughter, community. 'Where the Spirit of the Lord is', said Paul, 'there is liberty'. Such games aren't an escape or an irrelevance, for they help to humanize the world. Office parties, works outings, club teas — all can have an impact. They help us to see those whom we have to deal with for most of the time in an official capacity, as fellow humans. And on such occasions, when there is a spirit of carefree playfulness, we share in God's creative zest.

O God, bless all those who are care-worn and burdened. Grant them and us to know that carefree delight from which all things spring forth and to whom all things are moving.

HINTS OF GLORY

I think all of us are aware at times of being moved by strange feelings—feelings we find almost impossible to talk to anyone else about, feelings which are very difficult to put into words at all. They usually come when looking at something in nature—the evening sun setting over the sea, a large oak whose leaves are rustling in a breeze, fields and hills stretching to the horizon, a garden of flowers or even a single blossom. At such times we want to say something. 'Isn't it . . .' we begin. But how to go on? The word 'pretty' is totally inadequate. The word 'beautiful' is better but hardly seems strong enough. Perhaps we usually end up by saying something like, 'Isn't it marvellous' or 'Isn't it glorious'. Yet once again we are let down. It does make us marvel and glorify glory but the old phrases have been trundled out unthinkingly for so long they have lost their power. So, bearing in mind how inexpressible such experiences are, I will simply say that a glory seems to touch us—a glory which seems to have two aspects to it.

First, of course, it evokes a sense of wonder, amazement, marvel. Something sublime opens out before us evoking a mixture of delight and awe bordering on worship. Second, it also brings a tinge of sadness, almost a sense of pity or loss. What takes hold of us and takes us out of ourselves is somehow elusive, out of reach. There is a poem by Edward Thomas called simply, *The Glory*. It begins straightforwardly enough,

> The glory of the beauty of the morning
> The cuckoo crying over the untouched dew.

But throughout the poem there is a sense of something always just out of reach, leaving us at once exalted and unsatisfied. The last line of the poem puts it vividly: 'I cannot bite the day to the core.' It's almost as though we wanted to eat, to consume the universe, to make it become part of us but that this is impossible; we cannot bite the day to the core. C. S. Lewis believed that one day the glory of the universe would pass into us. He pointed to the biblical passages about God causing us to 'put on the splendour of the sun.' Now we discern the freshness and purity of the morning but they don't make us fresh and pure. We cannot mingle with the pleasures we see but one day it will be different and 'we will put on the glory of which nature is only a first sketch. We will receive it into ourselves, bathe in it, become part of it.' Perhaps this is what Paul was getting at when he said that, 'We, beholding the glory of the Lord, are being changed into his likeness from one degree of glory into another.'

But before I let myself get carried away by all this I will pull my own chair away and sit on the ground with a bump. Today some of you will be seeing people in geriatric wards or people who have been in mental hospitals for a long time or people besotted by drink or others whose physical state reflects in some way an inner defeat. It can make us very depressed. Is this honestly what God made a whole universe for? Millions and millions of years of evolution to the pinnacle of a senile mind staring blankly at a wall? There is of course no answer. Sometimes things seem very badly botched and we don't know God's reasons for this or why he thought it worth while to create in the first place. We live with a tension and with faith as our only guide. But this faith is based on something real — amongst other things on those hints of glory.

Grant us, O God, a vision of your glory, your glory in us, and in those whom we shall meet this day, through Jesus Christ our Lord.

The Faithful Witness
of your Saints in Every Age

CAEDMON

People who live in London and the south east sometimes kid themselves that this is the hub of the universe—the place where it's at, as they say, where everything important takes place. But this is foolish. For two hours after you get out of the train, Bristol or Birmingham or Huddersfield or Liverpool or wherever you live becomes the centre. And 1200 years ago, in the 7th century, London certainly wasn't the place where it was happening. It was from the far north west and the north east that new streams of Christian life were flowing into semi-pagan Britain.

One of my favourite people from that time, a man who was venerated as a saint in Jarrow and whose feast is kept in February, was called Caedmon. He was a farm labourer who like nearly every one else in those days was unable to read or write. He also seems to have been a little self-conscious and lacking in confidence, because when his friends got together after work sitting round the fire singing songs and entertaining one another Caedmon slipped away whenever the harp was offered to him. On one such occasion when he had slipped away and gone to the stable to look after the animals he fell asleep and had a dream. According to Bede, the first learned

Englishman and the historian from whom we learn about this period, a man came and stood beside Caedmon and said, 'Caedmon, sing me a song.' 'I don't know how to sing' he replied, 'it's because I can't sing that I left the feast and came here.' But the visitor persisted, 'You shall sing to me'. 'What shall I sing about?' Caedmon replied. 'Sing about the creation of all things' the other answered. And Bede goes on to say that Caedmon immediately began to sing verses in praise of God the creator that had never been heard before and which, roughly translated, go 'Let us sing how the eternal God, the author of all marvels, first created the heavens for the sons of men as a roof to cover them and how their almighty protector gave them the earth for their dwelling place.'

In the morning when Caedmon told his friends about his experience he was taken to see Hilda the abbess of the monastery for which he worked and all recognized that he had received a marvellous gift. He was invited to join the community and for the rest of his life he devoted himself to composing verses based on the biblical stories in the language of the people. As Bede wrote, 'He could quickly turn whatever passage of Scripture was explained to him into delightful and moving poetry in his own English tongue. These verses stirred the hearts of many folk to despise the world and aspire to heavenly things. Others after him tried to compose religious poems in English but none could compare with him, for he received this gift of poetry as a gift from God.'

Caedmon was an unlettered man whose gift came out of the blue. Few people have such a strong experience. But if Paul is to be believed we do all have a gift of one kind or another. As he wrote to the Ephesians 'Each of us has been given his gift, his due portion of Christ's bounty.' The future of the Christian faith depends upon each one of us, discovering just what this gift is and putting it to work in God's service. 'Each of us has been given his gift,' said Paul.

Thank you God for all those whose talents have enhanced life. Help each one of us to discover our own particular gift and to put it to work in the service of others.

PATRICK

Your eye catches a newspaper headline 'Confessions of a film star'. You expect to read about scandals, sex, the indiscretions of the famous. As your eye goes down the column you are not surprised; every salacious detail is there. But I want to talk about a rather different kind of confession. It was written over 1,500 years ago, about the year 450. We have a remarkable link with this confession, for in Dublin there is a book that's over 1,000 years old and the writer of this book says he copied the handwriting of St. Patrick himself. Patrick's home may have been near Dumbarton in Scotland. What is certain is that at the age of sixteen he was captured by a raiding party and carried off to Ireland. Like most people of that age Patrick wasn't particularly religious, but he changed. 'After I had come to Ireland', he wrote, 'I daily used to feed cattle, and I prayed frequently during the day; the love of God and the fear of him increased more and more, so that in one day I said about 100 prayers and in the night nearly the same.'

About six years later Patrick managed to escape and after various vicissitudes reached home. You might have expected him to breathe a sigh of relief and settle down. But a call came: 'I thought in my mind that I heard the voice of those who were near the wood of Foclut, which is close by the western sea. And they cried out thus as if with one voice, "We entreat thee, holy youth, that thou come, and henceforth walk among us".' So despite the tears of his family he went—went to work amongst the heathen Irish as they then were, whose slave he had so recently been. He preached the gospel, founded Christian churches and wrote his confession—not as people do today to make money but to confess his faith, to praise the Lord who had been so good to him.

Patrick was very conscious of his unworthiness, indeed of his complete unsuitability. Having missed so much schooling he worried that his Latin style was very simple. But above all he had a sense of the loving purpose of God who had taken hold of him, guided and strengthened him and who through him had brought knowledge of Christ to the Irish. He wrote, 'There was I, first a rustic, a fugitive, unlearned, indeed not knowing how to provide for the future—but I know this most certainly, that before I was humbled I was like a stone lying in the deep mud; and he who is mighty came, and in his own mercy raised me, and lifted me up and placed me on the top of the wall. And hence I ought loudly to cry out, to return also something to the Lord for his so great benefits, here and in eternity, which benefits the mind of men cannot estimate.'

Patrick belongs to all Irish Christians, both protestant and catholic. Indeed he belongs to us all. For his sense of life, shaped and strengthened by a good God, is open to everyone. Here is part of his famous breastplate,

Christ in the heart of every man who thinks of me,
Christ in the mouth of every man who speaks to me,
Christ in the eye of every man that sees me,
Christ in the ear of every man that hears me.

MARY, THE MOTHER OF THE LORD

If you had to take a friend to the loveliest sight you know, I wonder where you would go. Perhaps it would be to some lakes or mountains, to a well-kept garden or to a panorama of neat English fields. One of the places I would certainly think of taking my friend would be to the National Gallery in Trafalgar Square — in through the door and then left into the room of Italian paintings of the fifteenth century. There I might single out a painting by Fra Filippo Lippi. Lippi was a monk but apparently the life wasn't for him because after a while he was released from his vows and allowed to marry. But not before it was discovered he could paint and in the Gallery hangs his picture of the annunciation. It depicts the virgin Mary sitting in a chair, leaning slightly forward, head gently bowed. Before her is an angel, kneeling in humility, eyes open and full of deep feeling. The picture has a gentle, serene mood; an atmosphere of reverence, courtesy and tender love. You may have seen a Christmas card of it or one like it for Lippi's picture became the model for nearly all paintings of the annunciation.

I suspect that when the poet Edwin Muir was in Rome it was a picture like Lippi's that once moved him so much. Muir was brought up in the Orkneys with a somewhat severe Calvinism. One of his great delights later in life in rediscovering Christianity was to discover Christian art for the first time; the faith expressed not just in words as he remembered it as a child, but through symbols. 'I remember stopping for a long time one day,' he wrote, 'to look at a little plaque representing the annunciation. An angel and a young girl, their bodies inclined towards each other, their knees bent as if they were overcome by love, gazed upon each other'. Later he wrote a poem on the annunciation in which he pictures the angel and Mary gazing into each other's eyes in a deepening trance as if the gaze would never break. All around life goes on, familiar noises, lengthening shadows, but here, between the angel and Mary, is a moment of eternity.

Painters, poets and ordinary people in every age have been drawn to the scene of the annunciation. Its sheer loveliness has brought out the loveliest in us. But why, I wonder, does this story have such universal appeal? Is it because in the picture of the angel and Mary we have a symbol of the ideal relationship between God and every human soul? The angel says to Mary, 'Hail, thou that art highly favoured, the Lord is with thee.' The angel communicates to Mary the good news we want to believe but cannot quite bring ourselves to believe fully: that God wants our good, that he wants it more strongly than we want it ourselves; that God is for us and with us. In response Mary says quite simply, 'Behold, the handmaid of the Lord—be it unto me according to thy word.' Mary makes herself available; she gives an unreserved assent to God's purposes for her. The flow from heaven to earth and then back from earth to heaven is unbroken. God and man are in a communion of love.

The story of Mary has all the magic beauty of a fairy tale—with one big difference. She actually lived and lived out the Lord's will for her. And I know people—old people, middle-aged people, young people—whose lives have something of the quality of that annunciation scene; lives in which through the struggles, pressures, tensions and hopes of each day, we get a glimpse of heaven and earth at one.

Thank you God, for the gentle, serene beauty of the annunciation scene as depicted by painters and poets.
May we, like Mary, be so open to your grace, that we live in an unbroken communion of love with you and others, through Jesus Christ our Lord.

ANSELM

The other day someone came to see me to tell me that, as she put it, she had become a proper Christian for the first time in her life. Things had really changed for her and she was full of enthusiasm for her new found faith. I find it a puzzle, and perhaps you do too, that some people believe so strongly and others find it impossible to believe at all. I don't think this is simply a matter of brain power, as though the believer is clever and the non-believer stupid (or vice versa) for you can neither prove nor disprove the reality of God. All arguments leave the question open. Nor is it a question of one kind of person being good and the other bad. There are some nasty believers and some marvellous agnostics; and this is true the other way round as well.

Someone once suggested that having or not having faith is like looking at one of those pictures in which you can see two objects. One moment you see a vase for example. You blink your eye and then the same picture seems like two faces looking at each other. There's no particular reason why you should see one object rather than the other. So one person sees life in terms of God and another person doesn't. There's no way of proving which interpretation is correct and both are possible. This doesn't mean however that faith is just a matter of personal whim. Many philosophers tell us we can't prove that a real world exists outside our minds but nevertheless our whole life is lived on the assumption that there is one.

21st April is St. Anselm's day. He was a person who in 1093 became Archbishop of Canterbury and who in some people's opinion is the best one we've ever had. Anselm taught two things about faith which are still of fundamental importance. First, you can't be neutral about religion. You either believe or you are outside belief. It used to be fashionable in some quarters to think you could simply leave young children to make up their own minds about religion. Most modern parents now treat this view as the nonsense it is. Whether we like it or not we give our children a bias in favour of Christianity or a bias against it. We either bring up our children to know from the inside what it is to pray to and worship God or we leave them out in the cold. Faith must come first. Reasoning comes later.

So Anselm begins his famous discussion on why God became man by saying 'Those who make this request do not expect to come to faith through reason, but they hope to be gladdened by the understanding and contemplation of the things they believe.' This leads on to Anselm's second great emphasis. Genuine faith is always a faith that thinks. An unthinking faith is no faith at all. Faith for him is always *fides quarens intellectum* (faith seeking understanding). Of course we are not all thinkers. But we could put it like this. Do we use our brains to try and understand God and his purposes for us as much as we use our brains in our favourite hobby? So there never can be a proof or disproof of the Christian view of life but, given a basic faith, we are all of us seekers after a deeper understanding. I like it when Anselm says to those who have asked for his teaching, 'I shall try to the best of my ability, not so much to show you something as to search with you—with the help of God and your prayers.' A good attitude I think not just for an outstanding archbishop but for all of us. Here is a prayer of St. Anselm,

Grant, O Lord God, that we may cleave to thee without parting, worship thee without wearying, serve thee without failing, faithfully seek thee, happily find thee, for ever possess thee, the one only God, blessed world without end.

COLUMBA

Off the west coast of Scotland is the tiny island of Iona. It's hardly three miles by two, open to the winds and waves of the Atlantic. It was to here, in the year 563, that Columba sailed from his home in Ireland. No one knows quite why he came. One story says he got in a quarrel, was chucked out of the church, and to show he was sorry said he would win three thousand heathen souls for Christ. Others suggest that Columba, like all Celtic monks simply sought a place of solitude to be more alone with God. Anyway, to Iona he came and we can picture him there with his fellow monks collecting twigs to build their huts, fishing from their frail coracles, drying the harvest and doing all the other things necessary to stay alive. But also copying books from the Bible, (Columba is said to have copied over 300) and, most important of all, coming together every three hours to worship God and pray for the needs of mankind. The monks were also missionaries whose particular achievement was to bring the Christian faith to the Picts north of the Grampian mountains. Columba journeyed to Inverness to teach King Brude and it was from this tiny island that Christianity in Scotland really got going. For Scottish Christians the names Columba and Iona are very special.

But what kind of a man was Columba? It's not easy to find out. When people wrote the life of a saint in those days what interested them was the number of miracles they did. Our interests are rather different. There is some evidence that Columba was a man of strong passions and not just good ones. He may have been warlike, even vindictive on occasions. On the other hand like other Celtic saints he had an affinity with animals and there is an account of him rescuing a hurt crane on one of the beaches. Another story tells how he caught a robber stealing young seals from the seal farm. Columba didn't just remind him that stealing was wrong. He gave him some sheep so that he wouldn't starve. Certainly by the end of his life his natural ferocity seems to have been transformed.

Adamnan, who wrote Columba's life story, gives a lovely picture of his last days. Knowing he would die shortly Columba went round the island to say goodbye and bless his companions. When a tired old pack horse came whinnying up to him and someone tried to shoo it away Columba said to this brute beast, devoid of reason, 'the Creator himself hath evidently in some way made it known that its master is going to leave it.' Columba blessed the horse. He then went and did some copying, and stopped at the verse in Psalm 33 which reads, 'They that seek the Lord shall want no manner of thing that is good'. In the early hours of 9th June 597 he died. Those present described the scene in these words,

> The saint, even before his soul departed, opened wide his eyes and looked round him from side to side, with a countenance of wonderful joy and gladness, no doubt seeing the holy angels coming to meet him. A companion raised the right hand of the saint, that he might bless his assembled monks. And the venerable father himself moved his hand at the same time, as well as he was able. After his soul left the tabernacle of the body, his face still continued ruddy and brightened in a wonderful way by his vision of the angels and that to such a degree that he had the appearance not so much of one dead as of one alive and sleeping.

Thank you God for your saints.
Give us something of their faith and their hope in the face of death.
Bless Scotland, her church and her people.

THOMAS MORE

If you were given the job of designing the perfect person
I wonder how he would turn out. Suppose for example
instead of having to choose ten discs for your lonely
desert island you had to choose an ideal companion,
what qualities would you pick? I imagine we would all
agree that the person must have a sense of humour. It
would be terrible to live with someone incapable of
laughing or sharing a joke. And this isn't just because
people who can laugh with us are fun but because a
sense of humour is essential for keeping things in
perspective. People who can't laugh usually take themselves too seriously. Then I would want someone with
something up top. They wouldn't have to be highly
educated but they would have to be capable of thinking
for themselves. We would of course want our
companion to be kind but I think we would also agree
that there is more to goodness than a warm heart; we
would want them to have some steel to them, some guts.
We don't want them to go to pieces or collapse in a heap
of self-pity.

Then finally a quality that not everyone would value. I
would design the ideal companion to be a holy
person—a person who had a secret inner life that was
deep and close to God. People who are labelled religious
usually turn out to be the best or the worst people we
know—this is because what is highest in human life can
turn out terrible if it is even the slightest bit distorted.
But if a person really is close to God they often seem to
have a special something that is very attractive and very
necessary for that desert island; for after all when you
have made yourself comfortable and eaten your
coconuts and swum and sunbathed what is your life
actually going to be about? A holy person would be a
reminder that life is meant to be a spiritual journey into

ever deeper layers of truth. That then is my ideal companion—a person capable of laughing, particularly at themselves; able to rub two thoughts together, warm hearted with a tough core, and finally the quality we wouldn't all agree about, holiness.

The pity is that there isn't anyone with this combination of qualities—but I can think of one person who comes pretty near to it. Everyone agreed he had a marvellous sense of humour which came out not only with his family who adored him but even when he was approaching death. He joked to the man who gave him a helping hand onto the scaffold: 'When I come down again let me shift for myself as well as I can.' And to the person about to cut off his head he said, 'I forgive you but you'll never get any credit for striking off my head, my neck is so short.' He was one of the cleverest men of his time and the most learned men in Europe wanted to be his friend. One of them, Erasmus, said of him, 'He seems born and created for friendship.' But he was also a man of steel. After long careful thought he decided not to go along with unhappy, nasty Henry VIII. Even though his family didn't really understand what he was on about and even though his beloved daughter Meg had signed the oath, Thomas More believed that a crucial issue of principle was at stake. And despite long trials, the threat of torture, the thought of which terrified More, and the knowledge of certain death, he stood firm. Finally More was above all a man of God with his priorities absolutely right. 'The king's good servant,' he said to Henry once, 'but God's first.' Every Friday he spent by himself in meditation and prayer. 'He prays', wrote Erasmus, 'at set hours and he prays from the heart.' A marvellous person to share a desert island with and one for whose life many Christians give thanks. I end with part of a prayer Thomas More wrote for his own use whilst in the tower.

Give me, good Lord, a humble, lowly, quiet, peaceable, patient, charitable, kind, tender and pitiful mind, with all

*my works and all my words and all my thoughts to have a
taste of the holy blessed Spirit.*
*. . . a love to thee, good Lord, incomparable, above the
love to myself.*

FRANCIS

It is said that once when Francis was on his travels he
came on a village that was being terrorized by a wolf.
The woodcutters hardly dared to go to work, and at night
the inhabitants boarded up their windows. Much to the
dismay of the villagers Francis set off alone and
unarmed to the wolf's lair. Sure enough, on a narrow
path, he met the wolf but stood his ground unafraid.
Francis and the wolf then worked out some agreement
whereby the villagers were to leave food out and the
wolf would give up terrorizing them. In years to come, so
we are led to understand, the wolf became quite a
favourite in the village. How much truth there is behind
this legend of Francis we do not know. But it is charac-
teristic of his great love for nature and animals. Stories
abound of him preaching to the birds, and of his
attempts to persuade people to provide food for them at
Christmas.

Animals are a controversial subject. Some people
spend all their time and energy working for animal
causes. Others feel that the vast amount of human
misery ought to take priority. But let's begin behind this

controversy. Why are there animals in the first place? Perhaps like me you have a cat or some other pet, and you have looked at it and wondered—wondered what goes on behind those inscrutable eyes. Can a cat feel or think? Is there any reason for its existence? For many centuries men have believed that animals were created by God for the use of men. We have needed them to work our fields, carry us, hunt for us, and above all for food. Some modern thinkers have suggested a rather modified view of this. According to them, in order that our freedom over against God might be preserved, God created us at a kind of distance of knowing from himself, as part of a material universe; and animals form an essential part of the chain between stones and gases and ourselves as freely moving, thinking beings. Animals are an essential part of the conditions for bringing about independent human life.

But this is only one aspect of the truth. There is another—animal life has an intrinsic worth. It is valuable in itself. There is today a great deal of talk, writing and activity on behalf of the preservation of species that are in danger of dying out—certain kinds of whales, rare birds and so on. Why? On the face of it this hardly seems a very rational thing to do, when there are already so many different kinds of animals in the world. Perhaps it is because we recognize that the great multiplicity and variety of animal life has value in itself. There is an old myth, going back to Plato, which said that God, out of the inexhaustible fullness of his being, as it were poured out an endless variety of life in a great cascade. When bird lovers go to such lengths to preserve rare species and receive widespread support for this, we are implicitly recognizing the intrinsic worth of God's infinitely varied and rich cascade of being.

Animals then are not just here for men. They are God's creatures, with certain rights. In plain terms this means that when animals are involved, economic factors and human happiness cannot be the only considerations.

This is a fact embedded in the common moral conscious-ness of the country, and in our laws, and there is much to be desired in both. A distinguished committee set up a few years ago to investigate animal welfare said amongst many other things, 'Any animal should have sufficient freedom of movement to be able without difficulty to turn round, groom itself, get up, lie down and stretch its limbs. Adequate food and drink must be provided. Animals are likely to suffer from solitary confinement . . .' and so on. How all this is to be translated into practise is for those who know about such things. But the moral and theological point is crystal clear. Animals are God's creatures; an aspect of the infinite variety and richness of his creativity. They have certain rights.

O God, creator of heaven and earth, we bless your holy name for the wonder and mystery of animal life, and the enrichment this has been to human beings.

CECILIA

St. Cecilia was a girl who lived in Rome in the 2nd or 3rd century and who was killed for her love of Christ. Cecilia is usually depicted playing the organ and she has become the patroness of church music. I want to think about music, not only because of her but because music plays such a large part in so many people's lives. Indeed for many people music has taken the place of religion. Their strongest feelings, most painful longings, most exultant moments — all the very stuff of worship— are evoked by listening to records or going to concerts. But this religious dimension of music isn't just for those on the fringe of the churches. One of the most passionate and prophetic Christians of the 19th century, Kierkegaard, said, 'I owe everything to Mozart'. And the person whom many judge to have been the most distinguished theologian since Thomas Aquinas, namely Karl Barth, wrote also of Mozart that he was 'pure in heart' and that he 'knew more than the real fathers of the church or the reformers'.

Music, even for the expert and certainly for the musically illiterate like myself, is a great mystery, isn't it? Obviously it is more than pleasing sounds. It isn't just noise organized in a particular way and though music often expresses and evokes intense emotion it isn't merely emotion. Music seems to say something but we can never put into words just what it is saying. It seems to take us beyond words. The composer Mahler once wrote, 'As long as my experience can be summed up in words, I write no music about it; my need to express myself musically . . . begins at the door which leads into the "other world" — the world in which things are no longer separated by space and time.' And a contemporary Christian, Ulrich Simon, has stated the same thought in these words, 'For me the D minor quartet and the G minor quintet of Mozart evoke in every bar the truth about God, but I do not know how to express the truth. Perhaps it is a *musical* truth, for what do words like "tragic" and "searing" mean even if I related them to my chosen bars, themes and developments? Rather these empty words are fulfilled by the music. We owe everything to Mozart because he has revealed the priority of music in theology.'

Music, then, seems to lead us into another world, to make us aware of the spiritual dimension, in a way that words so often fail to do. Recently Norman St. John Stevas joked that he was learning the harp in order to prepare himself for heaven. But it's interesting isn't it how in the Bible heaven seems above all a place of music. 'I heard a sound from heaven like the noise of rushing water and the deep roar of thunder; it was the sound of harpers playing on their harps. There before the throne . . . they were singing a new song' says a passage in the book of The Revelation. I love too that prayer of John Donne, 'Bring us, O Lord God, at our last awakening, to the house and gate of heaven, to enter into that gate and dwell in that house, where there shall be no darkness nor dazzling but one equal light; no noise nor silence but one equal music.'

Sometimes we get a hint, through human music, of this music of heaven. Recently I got in the car, switched on the radio and some music came on. In a few seconds it succeeded in conveying a sense of total and absolute 'alrightness'. It conveyed musically the conviction of Mother Julian that in the end 'all will be well and all manner of things shall be well.' The music, which turned out to be one of the Amen's from Monteverdi's *Mass* pointed to and conveyed a hint of some final resolution and triumph. It changed my day—as music so often transforms the way we feel about things.

Thank you, God, for music and all it means to people. May it lead us to the music of heaven.

THE COMMUNION OF SAINTS

Mahatma Ghandi was a great Indian leader who was much respected by men all over the world. Within his own country he was regarded by millions as a holy man, a real saint. Yet it was about him that the English novelist George Orwell said, 'All saints should be judged guilty until they are proved innocent.' This was not, I think, just a superficial witticism. It accords with what people feel and reveal in such remarks as, 'I'm sure Mr. So-and-so is a saint—but I don't think I would like to live with him.' We know that human behaviour is complex and ambiguous. Good people sometimes have streaks of hardness in them. So-called bad people sometimes display spontaneous qualities of goodness. A hopeless alcoholic, for example, can sometimes be very generous or affectionate.

On All Saints' Day the church gives thanks for all those who have enriched us by the quality of their lives. But it's a mighty puzzling thing to know just who the real saints are. Perhaps like me you sometimes have the feeling that the best saints have yet to be unearthed; obscure people known only to a few friends and to God. What I am sure of is that there are saints, and that what the church calls the communion of saints is a reality.

Scientists tell us that life has evolved over millions of years from basic matter to human personalities like you and me. First electrons, atoms and molecules. Then cells combining in ever more complex forms to produce fishes, reptiles and the whole teeming range of animal life, from dinosaurs to the apes and ourselves. The question arises whether we have seen the end of this process. There was the great leap upwards, as it were, when matter, like stones and gases, produced life. Then there was another great leap when human beings emerged capable of thinking, making moral choices and loving God. Is there to be another great leap? The

Christian faith says, yes, there is. The end of the creative process is not man as we now know him but the communion of saints: a community of persons utterly transparent to God, as Christ was. The communion of saints is the great reality towards which human life is directed and is being drawn.

I know that all this talk about saints can be rather off-putting. It will make some people think of those who become monks or nuns—those who do things which for most of us are neither appropriate or possible—for we are, most of us, caught up in the daily struggle to earn a living. We are beset by the problems and worries of the daily round. So let's take heart from some words found in the spiritual diary of Dag Hammersköld, the former Secretary General of the United Nations. 'In our time', he wrote, 'the road to holiness necessarily passes through the world of action.'

I myself find encouragement in the example and words of Dietrich Bonhoeffer whose life certainly wasn't cloistered. He spent his last years resisting the Nazis, plotting against Hitler, and then in prison with all the inner turmoil and fears that you and I would have in such a situation. On 18th July 1944 he wrote a letter containing these words, 'To be a Christian does not mean to be religious in a particular way, to cultivate some particular form of asceticism, but to be a man.' A few days later he wrote another letter containing these words. 'I am still discovering up to this very moment that it is only by living completely in this world that one learns to believe ... This is what I mean by worldliness—taking life in one's stride, with all its duties and problems, its successes and failures, its experiences and its helplessness. It is in such a life that we throw ourselves utterly into the arms of God and participate in his sufferings in the world.'

Like Bonhoeffer most of us have to live our lives very much in this world—no secluded retreat for us. Like him we can learn to believe; learn to throw ourselves utterly into the arms of God, learn to live with integrity, courage and joy. In this task we have the glorious communion of saints to point the way and help us by their prayers.

We rejoice, O God, at the faithful witness of your saints in every age, praying that we may share with them in your eternal kingdom.

Fare Forward, Voyagers

A QUICKNESS KISSED BY GOD

During a visit to the sea recently I did as I always do when walking along the beach—follow the line of debris left by the tide. I suppose there remains within me some schoolboyish hope that I will find some valuable treasure washed up or at least something interesting. But this time my mind tended to wander from the thought of treasure to the shoes, toys, broken spars and bottles as signs of unknown lives endlessly discarding and perishing; to the rocks and sand rubbed by oceans for millions of years. Some lines of Eliot where he uses the sea as an image of time the destroyer came to mind,

It tosses up our losses, the torn seine,
The shattered lobsterpot, the broken oar
And the gear of foreign dead men.

The passingness of all things. The older we get the more this seems to be the great fact which somehow we have to come to terms with. It's funny though how we have endless articles and programmes on how people keep slim, look beautiful, grow better vegetables and decorate their walls but not on how people come to terms with the fact that all is slipping away. Somehow we don't seem to be able to face it. My favourite recipe for mortality is that of the person in Graham Greene's novel, *Travels with My Aunt*, who knowing he had a year to live bought a house with 364 rooms and changed to a new one every day on the principle that continuous change makes time seem longer.

More seriously, I suppose there are two main approaches. The first is summed up in the words of the old song, 'I'm going to live, live live until I die.' I admire people who take this attitude. People who look the fact of mortality in the face and decide that rather than letting it get them down they are going to live each moment to the full. A view expressed in the *Rubaiyat of Omar Khayyam* by the man with his glass of wine and book of verse,

Ah take the cash and let the credit go,
Nor heed the rumble of a distant drum . . .
Ah make the most of what we yet may spend
Before we too into the dust descend.

The other main approach—the dominant one in all the great religions of the world—has concentrated on apprehending an eternal realm beyond the flux of things, an imperishable order beyond the reach of change and decay. There is a lovely evening prayer which expresses this approach well. 'Grant that we who are fatigued by the changes and chances of this fleeting world may repose upon thy eternal changelessness.' But though there is, I believe, an eternal order, I am not sure that it solves, or is meant to solve, the problem of time; not sure it stops the pain caused by all things passing.

I would like to quote a single line by the poet Henry Vaughan which doesn't offer an escape from time, or a solution, but which does perhaps succeed in uniting the approach of those determined to live every moment to the full and those who live in the perspective of eternity. Life, Vaughan wrote, is what none can express, 'a quickness which my God hath kissed.' This day will be over so quickly and against the background of evolution your life and mine is, as Conrad once put it, a 'rapid blinking stumble across a flick of sunshine'. Life is a quickness—we are all too well aware of that—but it is a quickness which God hath kissed. The moment which is our life has been blessed and embraced by God. It is there for us to affirm and embrace in response.

O God, source and ground of all creation, for the moment which is our life and for each moment of this day, we bless your holy name.

NOT YET THE WHOLE TRUTH

You may have wondered sometimes how doctors, nurses and others who are in daily contact with human suffering are able to cope with it emotionally. For when someone close to us is ill we get very involved and obviously those who are in continuous contact with the afflicted cannot get as involved with each person as we do with a member of our own family. There has to be a measure of detachment—enough at least to be able to think clearly and professionally about what is the best thing to do. But it is a mistake to believe that those who work with the afflicted are without strong feelings for them, as I discovered not long ago.

Talking to some people who worked in a very upsetting area of human need I remarked that I didn't think it was possible to do such work without some detachment. They replied that sometimes when a distressed family had left the room, it was not possible to hold in their own tears. Again, I once heard about the reaction of a children's department in a hospital when a very ill child came in. It's easy to think, 'Oh they have sick people coming in all the time—they must get used to it.' But when this child came in the whole department was sad, and some felt angry—angry that life should contain such things. As one member said, 'I could never be anything but an atheist.' And yet there are other people, equally close to human suffering, who somehow retain their faith.

There is a moving scene in a novel by Camus in which a town is stricken by plague. The central character is a non-believing doctor who gives himself unsparingly to work amongst the sick. The other main character is the priest, Father Panaloux. One night Dr. Rieux and Father Panaloux sit together by the bed of a dying child. The doctor becomes angry that a child should die and when the priest suggests that what they have seen is revolting because it passes our understanding and that perhaps we should love what we cannot understand the doctor replies, 'No, Father. I've a very different idea of love. And until my dying day I shall refuse to love a scheme of things in which children are put to torture.' A shade of disquietude crossed the priest's face. He was silent for a moment. Then, 'Ah, doctor,' he said sadly, 'I've just realized what is meant by grace.' He meant, I think, that despite everything there was some influence, some power, beyond him that kept him a believer—something that held him.

Someone once suggested that the religious believer is like a good detective who has a hunch that things aren't what they seem. The evidence points to a particular culprit but the detective has an intuitive sense that the real truth is different; that there is more to it than meets the eye. Those who are closely involved with human distress sometimes feel that the case against there being a good and wise God is overwhelming. The believer is a believer precisely because like the good detective he senses that this is not the whole truth—that things are not what they seem to be on the surface.

Graham Greene's novels reveal a high degree of awareness of sin and suffering. He himself admits to long periods of extreme depression. Yet he remains a Catholic and recently he gave one of the most remarkable statements of faith that I have come across. 'I have very few beliefs now,' he said, 'but I continue to have a certain faith. I have the faith that I am wrong. And that my lack of belief is my fault. And that I shall be proved wrong one day.' Few of us have such a mature faith as this — a faith that our lack of faith will be proved wrong. Yet in our different ways most of us do still have some kind of belief.

Lord, in our different, funny old ways, we believe — help our unbelief.

DISEMBARKING SOON

One day I had to go to Cambridge to preach a sermon. I settled myself in the railway compartment and shut my eyes the better to concentrate on getting my thoughts in order. Then two girls came in. They must have been about 17 — wavy hair covering half of their faces, puffing away in a rather self-conscious way at cigarettes. They started to chatter away about some party or other they had been to recently and I returned to my thoughts. Suddenly from out of their chatter I thought I heard the words, 'Oh, he was horrible — you know, fat and forty.' Goodness I thought to myself. I've been putting on rather a lot of weight lately and I'm already past forty and here we are already written off with such disdain by these talkative young moppets. No sooner have we taken our place as grown-ups at the table of life than there seem to be younger people crowding round at the end pushing us off our chairs. Why *is* life so short? Why can't we live for ever and ever? Some authors, like the person who wrote the book of Genesis suggest that we would have lived for ever if only mankind hadn't sinned—that death is a kind of punishment for sin. But this can't be true because mortality belongs to all animal life of which we are a part. When our forebears first became conscious of being human they found that they came into the world, lived for a period and died much like their pre-human ancestors.

The best answer I've heard to the question of why we live for only such a very short time is that this gives us a manageable span within which to shape our lives. If we had the prospect of living for ever and ever without any kind of break or interruption we would perhaps find it just too much, too bewildering. As it now is we have a fixed span to make something of. As we plan for the day, week or year, so we can try to think of our life as a whole. It offers a definite stage in which something can be accomplished—in which some personal growth can take place.

Inevitably in middle age our thoughts turn more frequently to the prospect of our own end. For this is the fact above all others that we have to reckon with. If we do take it into account it makes for a new freedom. This is what Malcolm Muggeridge once wrote,

> Now the prospect of death overshadows all others. I am like a man on a sea voyage nearing his destination. When I embarked I worried about having a cabin with a porthole, whether I should be asked to sit at the captain's table, who were the more attractive and important passengers. All such considerations become pointless when I shall so soon be disembarking. The world that I shall soon be leaving seems more than ever beautiful, especially its

remote parts. Those I love I can love even more, since I have nothing to ask of them but their love; the passion to accumulate possessions, or to be noticed and important, is too evidently absurd to be any longer entertained.

Malcolm Muggeridge suggests that the prospect of death can bring a new liberation. Shakespeare, in one of his finest sonnets, carries the thought even further. He begins,

Poor soul, the centre of my sinful earth
Why dost thou pine within and suffer dearth,
Painting thy outward walls so costly gay?
Why so large a cost, having so short a lease,
Dost thou upon thy fading mansion spend?

And ends,

Within be rich, without be rich no more.
So shalt thou feed on Death, that feeds on men,
And, Death once dead, there's no more dying then.

O God, help us to be so inwardly rich that we are released from the striving to have more things, to be noticed or important, and so freed also from the hold of death, through Jesus Christ our Lord.

TOO GOOD TO BE TRUE?

C. S. Lewis was one of the best known and most appreciated Christians of our time. For many years he was an atheist, and when he was converted to Christianity he always stood for a tough-minded version of the faith with no watering down. He married late in life—very happily. But after a tragically short time his wife died. In order to help himself come through the grief C. S. Lewis kept a notebook in the weeks after his wife's death. Every day he wrote down what he felt and thought. This was later published, at first under another name, with the title *A Grief Observed*. One of his jottings at that time reads, 'Talk to me about the truth of religion, and I'll listen gladly. Talk to me about the duty of religion, and I'll listen submissively. But don't come to me talking about the consolations of religion or I shall suspect that you don't understand.' He found that what he called the consolations of religion didn't console. At the top of his mind he believed in a life after death, but it wasn't a real comfort. It didn't get through to his feelings.

Quite a lot of other people have had a similar experience. I suspect that one of the reasons for this is the nagging doubt that the idea of heaven is only wishful thinking. Most people would like, so strongly, to believe that there is a life beyond death for the ones they love and for themselves, that we become suspicious of the belief. It seems almost too good to be true. Then most of us have been influenced in one way and another by Freud, who taught this. Life is hard, he said, and our unconscious spins a web of fantasy—that there is a good God and a life after death—to make it bearable. And of course Freud had a point. The tendency to wishful thinking in most of us is pretty strong. We are right to be on our guard. Not long ago the distinguished novelist and philosopher, Iris Murdoch, wrote 'All that consoles is fake'.

Frankly, I find this assertion rather difficult to answer; for the simple reason that the view of life offered by the Christian faith is so wonderful. If I had to sit down and do the impossible—invent the perfect religion from scratch—I think I would come up with something very like the Christian faith. What could be more glorious and encouraging than the idea that the universe is created by a loving wisdom; that this divine mind gives us freedom to build our own lives, but that he shares all our struggles, pain and hopes; that he has taken the supreme step of self-abandonment in uniting himself with human personality in Christ; that Christ's presence continues with us; that this life is not all there is, but a first stage of the journey towards a final consummation of unimaginable happiness. No wonder our suspicious modern minds carp and say it's all too good to be true. Yet hopes and dreams are not false just because they are hopes and dreams. Every famous footballer was once a boy dreaming of scoring fantastic goals. Every accomplished cricketer was once a boy whose mind was filled with cover-drives to the boundary. These dreams provided the motive power for hours of hard training and practice.

Some human imaginings are of course only fantasies. But others provide inspiration, incentive, and, yes, consolation. For Christians the human dream has become embodied in the specific promises of Christ.

Blessed are those who hunger and thirst for righteousness, for they shall be satisfied.

Blessed are the merciful for they shall obtain mercy.

Blessed are the pure in heart, for they shall see God.

Blessed are the peacemakers, for they shall be called sons of God.

These are definite promises—promises which can bring both hope and a renewed seriousness to become like God, in whose image we are made.

O God, grant us true hope, hope that inspires us to live fully and hope in the face of death.

READY TO GO

Living in retirement in a village by the Thames in a comfortable house embraced by a profusion of roses is Peggy Makins. Recently Peggy Makins was interviewed in connection with a book she has written and she came out with rather a surprising statement—a sentiment few people would admit to themselves let alone others. She said, 'I'm not grateful to be alive. I'll put up with it,' and she went on, 'I dreamt recently that I was going to die when I was 60—I'm 59 now—and my reaction was one of sheer relief.' My first reaction to this was one not only of surprise but of shock. After all, Peggy Makins was, according to the article, a religious woman; she said she believed in a loving God. How ungrateful I thought to be so begrudging about life and so pleased at the thought of dying.

And there came to mind two very different statements. One by Wordsworth who wrote to a friend in 1825, 'Theologians may puzzle their heads about dogmas as they will, the religion of gratitude cannot mislead us. I look abroad upon nature, I think of the best part of our species, I lean upon my friends, I meditate upon the scriptures, and my creed rises up of itself.' More recently Malcolm Muggeridge has written, 'A sense of enormous gratitude to my creator overwhelms me often. I believe that in all circumstances and at all times life is a blessed gift.' These are fine sentiments — gratitude for life — gratitude in all circumstances and at all times.

But recently, what two people have said to me, has made me think again. First, a person who has suffered much from a terrible disease told me she wished she was dead, and I could only sympathize very much with her feeling. Then another person, when I asked her how she felt in the morning, said that she looked forward to the coming day because it was that much nearer going. One person felt she had suffered enough. The other felt she had come to the end of a long and full life. And is their attitude so very wicked? After all there is some biblical support for it. Paul once said, 'For me to live is Christ, and to die is gain. My desire is to depart and be with Christ, for that is far better.'

Paul believed it was better to be dead than alive — few today have this degree of conviction and funnily enough even those who do believe that this life leads into something more spacious are almost afraid to talk about it for fear of being thought escapist. It was Freud who made us all a little hesitant. He once wrote an anti-religious passage in his splendid style, 'Of what use to man is the illusion of a kingdom on the moon whose revenues have never been seen by anyone? As an honest crofter on this earth he will know how to cultivate his plot in a way that will support him.' But there comes a point when the honest crofter who has cultivated his plot hard all day is thinking about home. He enjoys the walk back. He is grateful for the evening light and the sound of the birds closing the day. But he is tired and he looks forward to getting home. The Christian faith, if we will have it, offers hope at the end of the day. Trusting in God, united to Christ by compassionate action, prayer and sacrament, we can share Pope John's readiness. 'My bags are packed,' he said; 'I am ready to go.'

Thank you, good Lord, for the marvel of being alive.
Unite us this day to yourself and kindle in us hope for
what lies ahead, through Jesus Christ our Lord.

STRENGTHENED BY THEIR FELLOWSHIP

One thing that doesn't change very much is children's puzzles. I expect that you had, as I had, and children now still have, those books in which you draw a picture by joining one numbered dot to another. You don't know what the picture is meant to be until you've finished—that's part of the interest. You just have to go on following the numbers, joining up the dots, until the outline becomes recognizable. And there may come a time when you wonder just what, if anything, your joined up dots are going to turn into. A kangaroo or a hippopotamus? A stork or a walrus? You can't tell. And sometimes we get the same sense of puzzlement about living. We go on from day to day, joining one dot of time to another, but to what end? What's all this daily pain and effort leading to? Great grandfather is born and grows up and marries and has children and dies and grandfather grows up and marries and has children and dies and your parents grow up and get married and have children and that's you. As one of the biblical writers who often made himself depressed thinking like this said, 'Vanity of vanities. All is vanity.'

But a clue to where it's all leading can be obtained by looking at any object about us, however simple—a grain of sand, for example. A grain of sand is made up of smaller units, molecules, atoms and electrons which have come together to form that grain without losing their own identity; the electrons and atoms are still there. Or I look at my hand—millions and millions of cells—a miracle of complex functioning; but here again the cells are still there. In making my hand they don't cease to be. In nature individual units come together to form complex wholes and these complex units in turn combine to bring about more complex ones still until here we are, you and I and everyone else peering out of our minds wondering what it's all about.

The Christian faith says that this process of continuing creation hasn't yet stopped. Matter, life, mind, and then another step, another leap, to what the church calls the communion of saints: though this leap is really two leaps. For the order goes: matter, life, mind, then mind utterly transparent to God in Christ, and finally all minds transparent to God, as men become joined to Christ.

And the principle seen in nature applies to the communion of saints—the individual units remain, transfigured I'm sure beyond our wildest dreams but richly, intensely themselves within the fellowship of divine love. Generations come and generations go but those who choose can unite themselves to divine love and be taken into the communion of saints. It is not escapism to talk about the communion of saints but it is certainly easier to go on courageously and hopefully if we know that life is leading somewhere.

Bishop Joseph Hall was a moderate, and like most moderates was attacked from all sides. In 1621 he was sent to the tower. Later he was released but kicked out of his bishop's house at Norwich. He then lived in great poverty until his death. This is what he wrote about the saints,

Let no man think that because those blessed souls are out of sight and we are here toiling in a vale of tears, we have therefore lost all mutual regard to each other. No; there is still and ever will be, a secret and unfailing correspondence between heaven and earth. As for us wretched pilgrims that are yet left here below to tug with many difficulties, we cannot forget that better half of us that is now triumphant in glory. It is abundant comfort to us that our head and shoulders are above water while the other limbs are yet wading through the stream.

We give you thanks, O God, for those whose faith and love have made them part of your fellowship of saints. Give courage and hope to those finding it difficult to struggle on.

AS THE BLIND COMES DOWN

Some people feel that religion is anti-life, but properly understood there need be no antagonism between religion and life. For it is God who has made us physical beings and set us in a world which arouses and delights the senses. What we see and hear, taste, touch and smell is meant to be integrated into the life of faith. Yet having said this a problem of some anguish remains; one which we need to have out with God. 'You have created us, O God, as physical beings in a world which gives pleasure. We rejoice in the sunlight and the shadows, the sound of waves and the smell of lilac—and then you take it all away from us. Our eyesight fades, our hearing becomes hard, our memory less good, until finally the blind comes down over the window of our mind.' And the point is that though we might be quite willing to give up the most basic pleasures, like eating an ice cream or drinking a glass of cold lager on a hot day, our most profound and sustaining experiences, music, poetry, the sight of hills, friendships—all this too is taken away from us. And what, I wonder, does God reply?

Perhaps something like this. 'I take it away from you only to give you something better. All that pleases eye and ear does it not come from me? What you experience now is only a foretaste, a scent carried in the wind, an echo of an indescribable beauty. Know me and know a delight which never fades.' Yet still a nasty niggle remains, for the fact is that in practice trying to know God better seems so hard. Even the devout find it difficult on occasions to begin to pray and think it nice when they stop; worship too often seems a drag. Life around us is immediate and real. The world of colour, and sound pulls. Those who try to go beyond the immediate sensation to God from whom it comes find an effort has to be made. I don't know what God might say to this, except, 'Go on trying—persevere. The end is worth it and no one can make the journey for you.'

Yet one practical point can I think be made. All those who have wanted to know God better seem to have felt the need for time on their own. Christ went away into lonely desert places to pray; monks have sought solitary caves. I went once to give some talks to a group of holiday makers at the Othona community in a remote part of south east Essex. What an intriguing landscape. Flat fields for miles in one direction, flat sea for miles in the other and between them a sea wall that you can walk along for fifteen miles without seeing anyone—only the marshes and mudflats and the sun hanging like a vast ball in the unending sky.

It was here that in the year 653 St. Cedd came down from Lindisfarne in the north east to convert the East Saxons to Christianity and he built a chapel which still stands. Somewhat barn-like in structure now, built of a motley mixture of plain stones and old Roman brick, it encloses a silence impregnated with the stillness of God. It is a place where, to quote Eliot, 'prayer has been valid.' Three miles away there is a nuclear power station, vast and gaunt against the sky, and the throb and whine of revolving metal is carried across the fields. But the silence in the chapel speaks of a greater power than that unleashed by the splitting of atoms. Outside is the bleak mysterious beauty of flat earth and endless sky but the stillness of the chapel points beyond a beauty registered by the senses to that from which all beauty comes. Goodness knows it's difficult to get a moment's silence in the noisy urban life of today but when we do it isn't a negative thing. It's a space cleared in the jungle of sound for awareness to grow — awareness of what is given as our senses wear away.

O God, we rejoice in this world of light and colour, shape and sound, but lead us beyond it to know you from whom all good things do come.

LETTING GO

I hope you had a restful night's sleep. Sleep is an amazing thing isn't it? For seven or eight hours we are prepared to let go; to surrender all control over our mind and sink into a dream-filled darkness. When awake most of us are so anxious to keep everything under control. Yet, come the night, and we give ourselves up to the unknown. Some people find this threatening and difficult. I once went to see an extraordinary play by Samuel Beckett called, *Not I*. It only lasted for twenty minutes but it was so intense you couldn't have taken more. The stage was dark except for a pair of large lips covered in phosphorescent paint. Out of this mouth came a non-stop stream of frenzied speech. It filled the theatre and became literally unbearable. This stream of terrified talk came from the mind of a person becoming unconscious, either through drugs or because they were dying. As it went under the mind sensed dark figures gathering and became terrified.

We all have something of this fear—and not only about sleep or death. T. S. Eliot has some lines in which he says, 'Do not let me hear of the wisdom of old men, but rather of . . . their fear of possession, of belonging to another, or to others or to God.' We fear to belong to others because any relationship that is worth while is not completely under our control. It involves a kind of surrender, and we would rather keep buttoned up, ourselves to ourselves. We don't want to let ourselves in for anything we can't control even when people are kind. In a play about the last war, a man in hospital was slowly dying through kidney trouble. The rest of the ward knew this and wanted to surround and support him with love. But the dying soldier couldn't receive their kindness. Even when they offered him cigarettes he refused them with the words, 'I have my own.'

And if we fear to belong to others how much more do

we fear to belong to God. In his autobiography Graham Greene described how, although he had no religious belief, he wanted to marry a Catholic girl. To please her he took a course of instruction to find out what it was all about, though he had no intention of becoming a believer or of being received into the church. The person who instructed him had once been an actor in the West End, but God had called him to the priesthood. When Graham Greene heard about this he wrote that his story 'came like a warning hand placed on my shoulder. "See the danger of going too far." That was the menace it contained.' Be very careful. Keep well within your depth. There are dangerous currents out at sea which could sweep you anywhere.' Yet, against his natural inclination, he came to believe. But he described his emotions as he walked away from the baptism in these words: 'There was no joy in it at all, only a sombre apprehension. I had made the first move with a view to my future marriage, but now the land had given way under my feet and I was afraid where the tide would take me. Even my marriage seemed uncertain to me now. Suppose I discovered in myself what Father Trollope had once discovered, the desire to be a priest.'

If we want a reposeful sleep, if we want to die with peace of mind, if we want any rich relationships, if we want to believe in God, a kind of surrender is neces-sary—a letting go, a being prepared to be taken by the tide to where we do not know. The Christian faith says simply, 'Do not be afraid.' We let go into faithful hands. As a phrase in the Bible puts it, 'underneath are the ever-lasting arms.' When Christ died on the cross, according to Luke the last words he said were, 'Father into thy hands I commit my spirit.' This is the way to close our eyes in sleep or death. This is the way to face a difficult situation during the coming day. This is the way to begin the day itself.

Father into thy hands I commit my spirit.

AN HOUR TO BUILD

One of the delights of going to the sea-side is standing on the shore watching boats out at sea: white horses running on the surface, dinghys leaning into the wind, yachts heading out to the horizon. For many people such a scene sums up all that they mean by the word picturesque. But ships on the sea are more than a pretty picture. They arouse strong, complex emotions. For example if you are looking out on the English channel with a mist beginning to come down, the sound of an occasional fog horn and large shapes gliding mysteriously through the gloom, you feel strange. The sights and sounds combine to effect you powerfully in a way that is difficult to define. A less complex emotion aroused by ships, particularly by well designed six-berth yachts, is pure escapism. They symbolize the chance of getting away from it all—away from the pressures and responsibilities of every day to sunny untroubled relaxation. This was brought out very well in a film I once saw in which a young girl was shown standing on the shore looking out to sea at a beautiful yacht. In her mind the ship sailed, silently, effortlessly closer and closer to the shore, wafted her lightly on board and then glided away. Away from all the pain and muddle.

A person for whom the sight of ships aroused strong feelings like this was the painter Casper David Friedrich who lived in what is now East Germany at the beginning of the 19th century. Friedrich was a deeply religious man but instead of expressing his faith through the usual biblical subjects he painted landscapes—landscapes full of symbols of what he believed about life. His ideas are quite simple—decay and destruction all about us, inevitable death looming up just ahead and a longing hope for something better beyond. In a lesser artist such ideas could have become very banal, but Friedrich's pictures are disturbing and haunting: bare, gaunt trees with the sky lighting up beyond, ruins, solitary monks by the sea shore and so on. And ships for him were not just ships. In one of his pictures a woman is shown looking out of a window. All we see is her back view so we are, as it were, looking out of the window with her. Outside, masts of yachts are prodding up into the sky, and beyond is the light golden haze of a far shore and the encouraging blue of the sky. Those who know about his paintings tell us that the strip of water outside the window is the sea of death through which we all have to pass; the ship is the craft that will carry us across it and beyond is the light of immortality. The woman gazing out of the window is looking and longing. The first reaction of many of us today to this kind of religious faith is to accuse it of escapism. For Christianity is first and foremost about serving God in this world. But this world is not the only one there is. Here we build the ship that will bear us across the waters of death. This is how John Masefield saw it in a poem he called *Truth*:

Man with his burning soul
Has but an hour of breath
To build a ship of truth
In which his soul may sail—
Sail on the sea of death,
For death takes toll
Of beauty, courage, youth,
Of all but truth.

Stripped of all purple robes,
Stripped of all golden lies,
I will not be afraid,
Truth will preserve through death.
Perhaps the stars will rise—
The stars like globes
The ship my striving made
May see night fade.

Grant, O God, that in our praying, thinking and striving during this day we may build a ship of truth.

ACKNOWLEDGEMENTS

For permission to reprint copyright material I have to thank the following:

Faber and Faber Limited and the estate of C. S. Lewis for two short extracts from *A Grief Observed* by C. S. Lewis.

Curtis Brown Ltd. and the estate of C. S. Lewis for a short extract from *Letters to Malcolm* by C. S. Lewis (Collins, Fountain Books).

R. S. Thomas for some lines from 'The Dark Well' (published in *Tares* by Rupert Hart Davis), and some lines from 'Country Clergy' (published in *The Bread of Truth* by Rupert Hart Davis).

Philip Toynbee for a letter which originally appeared in *The Times*.

Gavin Muir and the Hogarth Press for two short extracts from *An Autobiography* by Edwin Muir.

Faber and Faber Limited for some lines from 'One Foot in Eden' from *Collected Poems 1921-1958* by Edwin Muir.

Malcolm Muggeridge for an extract from 'Credo', originally published in *The Observer*.

The Bodley Head and Graham Greene for a short extract from *A Sort of Life,* by Graham Greene.

The Society of Authors as the literary representative of the estate of John Masefield for 'Truth' by John Masefield.

The trustees of the Tagore estate and Macmillan, London and Basingstoke, for part of a prayer from *Collected Poems and Prayers* by Tagore.